1999 SUPPLEMENT

CASES AND MATERIALS

INTELLECTUAL PROPERTY

Trademark, Copyright and Patent Law

by

ROCHELLE COOPER DREYFUSS
Professor of Law
New York University School of Law

ROBERTA ROSENTHAL KWALL
Raymond P. Niro Professor of Intellectual Property Law
DePaul University College of Law

NEW YORK, NEW YORK
FOUNDATION PRESS
1999

 TEXT IS PRINTED ON 10% POST
CONSUMER RECYCLED PAPER

ACKNOWLEDGEMENTS

We would like to thank David O. Carson, General Counsel, U.S. Copyright Office, and Tanya M. Sandros, Attorney Advisor, U.S. Copyright Office, for their insight and assistance in connection with the recently enacted Digital Millennium Copyright Act.

*

TABLE OF CONTENTS

TABLE OF CASES

Principal cases are in bold type. Non-principal cases are in roman type. References are to Pages.

*

1999 SUPPLEMENT

INTELLECTUAL PROPERTY

Trademark, Copyright and Patent Law

*

ASSIGNMENT 2

REQUIREMENTS FOR TRADEMARK PROTECTION: USE: AS A SIGNAL, IN COMMERCE, AND INTERSTATE

PART A: REQUIREMENTS FOR REGISTRATION

NOTES

Insert on page 44, at the end of Note 6:

Later in the Supplement, a congressional experiment with protection for product configurations will be discussed, see Note 6 added to page 316, infra, on vessel hull legislation.

PART B: LIMITS ON REGISTRABILITY

Add on page 67 after Note 1 as Note 1a:

1a. *Domain names and telephone numbers.* Pursuant to a contract with the National Science Foundation, Network Solutions, Inc. (NSI) became the exclusive registrar of most Internet domain names. The existence of top-level domains such as ".com", ".edu", and ".gov" necessitates the invocation of exclusive second-level domain names appearing just to the left of the top-level domain names (e.g., merck.com; luc.edu). The commercial activity domain—".com"—is the largest and fastest growing, and more than 100,000 new commercial domain-name registrations are added each month.[1]

NSI's practice of registering such domain names on a "first-come/first served" basis, absent consideration of prior trademark ownership rights, has spawned significant litigation in recent years.[2] For example, in Planned Parenthood Federation of America v. Bucci,[3] the plaintiff, a non-profit, reproductive health care organization and holder of the Planned Parent-

---

[1] Peter H. Lewis, *Dropping an Internet Hot Potato*, N.Y. Times, June 8, 1998, § D, at 4.

[2] See generally Michael B. Landau, Problems Arising Out of the Use of "WWW.Trade-mark.Com": The Application of Principles of Trademark Law to Internet Domain Name Disputes, 13 Ga. St. U. L. Rev. 455 (1997).

[3] 42 U.S.P.Q.2d 1430 (S.D.N.Y. 1997).

hood mark, sued the defendant, who had registered the domain name "plannedparenthood.com" and used it as the address of a Web site promoting his anti-abortion book. The plaintiff sued based on service mark infringement, federal unfair competition, and federal dilution. The court issued a preliminary injunction against the defendant's using the plaintiff's Planned Parenthood mark to identify its web site, home page, domain name or any other Internet material. In so holding, the court found that because the defendant did more than simply register the domain name in that he also "created a home page that uses plaintiff's mark as its address, conveying the impression to Internet users that plaintiff is the sponsor of defendant's web site,"[4] there was a likelihood of confusion arising from the defendant's activity. Compare Juno Online Servs., L.P. v. Juno Lighting, Inc.[5] (holding that registration of a trademark as a domain name is not use of the trademark on the Internet in connection with goods or services and is not prohibited by § 43(a)) *with* Lockheed Martin Corp. v. Network Solutions, Inc.,[6] (noting that the reasoning of *Juno* applies even more strongly regarding NSI because it did not register domain names resembling plaintiff's service mark for its own use but "merely accepted domain name registrations from others").[7] For a brief discussion of domain names and trademark dilution, see the section in this Supplement on Assignment 3, Part B.

A connection exists between the issue raised in *Dial–A–Mattress* and domain names in that courts show an inclination to enjoin confusingly similar uses of both types of subject matter based on principles of trademark and unfair competition law. Vanity telephone numbers and domain names are similar in that both facilitate the connection of one machine to another machine, and both are valuable to trademark holders by facilitating location of the trademark holder. Therefore, when the holder of a vanity telephone number, as well as a domain name holder, promotes this subject matter in a way that is likely to cause consumer confusion, infringement will result.[8]

As of 1996, NSI has maintained a policy of requiring applicants for domain names to warrant that their use of their desired domain name does not interfere with others' intellectual property rights. According to NSI's policy, if a trademark holder presents NSI with a trademark registration of a trademark identical to a currently registered domain name, NSI will cancel the domain name registration unless the holder can prove that it has a pre-existing right to use the domain name.

It is, however, doubtful that this policy or the case law set out above will continue in effect. In 1998, the Commerce Department, after a series of

---

[4] Id. at 1437.

[5] 979 F.Supp. 684, 44 U.S.P.Q.2d 1913, 1919–20 (N.D. Ill. 1997).

[6] 985 F.Supp. 949, 44 U.S.P.Q.2d 1865 (C.D. Cal. 1997).

[7] Id. at 1873.

[8] See *Lockheed Martin*, 44 U.S.P.Q. at 1872.

local and international negotiations, created the Internet Corporation for Assigned Names and Numbers (ICANN) which is to take over the administration of domain registrations, and thus all of NSI's functions.[9] ICANN's goal is to introduce competition in the administration of domain name registrations. Its first action, undertaken as this Supplement is being prepared, is to test competition through the appointment of five companies, which will be authorized to receive and process applications for domain name registrations in the .com, .net and .org domains, pursuant to a set of guidelines that ICANN is now in the process of vetting. By the end of June 1999, 29 additional companies are expected to be accredited.

The clash between trademark rights and domain names will be dealt with in these guidelines, through procedures that ICANN is developing in conjunction with the World Intellectual Property Organization (WIPO). After first releasing an interim paper indicating its thoughts on how to resolve the clash, WIPO recently issued a Final Report in the form of recommendations to ICANN. Among other things, the executive summary of WIPO's Final Report reads as follows:[10]

(i) The adoption of a number of improved, standard practices for registrars with authority to register domain names in the generic top-level domains (gTLDs)[including .com, .org. and .net] will reduce the tension that exists between domain names and intellectual property rights.

(ii) In particular, the collection and availability of accurate and reliable contact details of domain name holders is an essential tool for facilitating the protection of intellectual property rights on a borderless and otherwise anonymous medium. Such contact details provide the principal means by which intellectual property owners can go about the process of enforcing their rights.

* * *

(v) ICANN should adopt a dispute-resolution policy under which an administrative dispute-resolution procedure is made available for domain name disputes in all gTLDs. In the Interim Report, it was recommended that domain name applicants should be required to submit to the procedure in respect of any intellectual property dispute arising out of a domain name registration. The Final Report recommends that the scope of the administrative procedure be limited to cases of bad faith, abusive registration of domain names that violate trademark rights ("cybersquatting," in popular terminology). Domain name holders would thus be required to submit to the administrative procedure only in respect of allegations that they are involved in

---

[9] Information about ICANN can be found at its website, *www.icann.org*. NSI continues to administer domain names until ICANN's actions actually go into effect.

[10] The full proposal and a history of the domain name problem is available (in English) at *http://wipo2.wipo.int/process/eng/processhome.html*.

cybersquatting, which was universally condemned throughout the WIPO Process as an indefensible activity that should be suppressed.

(vi) The administrative procedure would be quick, efficient, cost-effective and conducted to a large extent online. Determinations under it would be limited to orders for the cancellation or transfer of domain name registrations and the allocation of the costs of the procedure (not including attorneys' fees) against the losing party. Determinations would be enforced by registration authorities under the dispute-resolution policy.

(vii) Famous and well-known marks have been the special target of predatory and parasitical practices on the part of a small, but active, minority of domain name registrants. A mechanism should be introduced whereby the owner of a famous or well-known mark can obtain an exclusion in some or all gTLDs for the name of the mark where the mark is famous or well-known on a widespread geographical basis and across different classes of goods or services. The effect of the exclusion would be to prohibit any person other than the owner of the famous or well-known mark from registering the mark as a domain name.

(viii) The exclusion mechanism gives expression in cyberspace to the special protection that is established for famous and well-known marks in the Paris Convention for the Protection of Industrial Property and the TRIPS Agreement.

(ix) Since an exclusion would cover only the exact name of the famous or well-known mark, and since experience shows that cyber-squatters typically register many close variations of famous or well-known marks, an exclusion, once granted, should give rise to an evidentiary presumption in the administrative procedure. The effect of the evidentiary presumption would to place the burden of proving justification for the use of a domain name on the domain name holder where the domain name is identical or misleadingly similar to the famous or well-known mark and the domain name is being used in a way that is likely to damage the interests of the owner of the mark.

Insert on page 68, directly under the dog:

In a 145–page opinion citing social science and historical research, along with standard legal analysis, the Trademark Trial and Appeal Board canceled six marks belonging to the Washington Redskins on the ground that material utilizing the word "Redskins" (and also a caricature) "disparage Native Americans and may bring them into contempt or disrepute." The parties seeking cancellation also suggested that the marks were scandalous, but the Board did not agree with this ground. As of this writing, the opinion, Harjo v. ProFootball, Cancellation #21,069, is available only at the PTO's website.[11] The cancellation does not, of course,

---

[11] http://www.uspto.gov/web/offices/com/sol/foia/tab/2aissues/1999/21069.pdf

directly affect the decision whether to continue to use the name "Red-skins" for a football team.

Insert on page 71, after Note 8:

8a. *Consumer standing.* There has been controversy over the question whether individuals (as opposed to competitors) have standing to oppose registration. On the one hand, § 1063 of the Act gives the right to "any person who believes that he would be damaged." On the other hand, federal law generally limits rights of-action to those directly affected by the activity that is the focus of the claim.[12] In Ritchie v. Simpson,[13] the Federal Circuit articulated a "real interest" test. In that case, William B. Ritchie, a member of the public, opposed Orenthal James Simpson's application to register the marks O.J. SIMPSON, O.J., and THE JUICE for use with a broad range of goods, including figurines, trading cards, sportswear, medallions, coins, and prepaid telephone cards. The opposition claimed that the marks were either immoral or scandalous matter or primarily merely a surname. The Trademark Trial and Appeal Board ("Board") dismissed, holding that Mr. Ritchie did not have standing. The Federal Circuit reversed. First, the court noted that standing before an administrative agency is broader than the standards adopted under Art. III of the Constitution for standing before federal courts. Second, it argued that the issue of immorality and scandalousness are ones on which public input is especially important. Under its "real interest test," the opposer must "have a legitimate personal interest in the opposition" and he or she must reasonably believe in the claim of potential injury. Thus, Mr. Ritchie's allegations—that he would be damaged by the registration of the marks because the marks disparage his values, especially those values relating to his family—were enough to create standing. And this was true even though his fears about giving federal protection to marks arguably "synonymous with wife-beater and wife-murderer," might be widely shared. The court sent the case back to the PTO to determine whether, in fact, these marks violate the standards of the statute.

[12] See, e.g., Sierra Club v. Morton, 405 U.S. 727, 92 S.Ct. 1361, 31 L.Ed.2d 636 (1972).

[13] 170 F.3d 1092 (Fed. Cir. 1999).

ASSIGNMENT 3

THE SCOPE OF THE TRADEMARK HOLDER'S RIGHTS: INFRINGEMENT AND CONTRIBUTORY INFRINGEMENT

PART A: COMPETING GOODS

NOTES

Add on page 116, as a second paragraph to Note 2e:

The Third Circuit visited the issue of standing under § 43(a) in Conte Bros. Automotive, Inc. v. Quaker State–Slick 50 Inc.,[1] a false advertising action brought by a nationwide class of retail sellers of motor oil and other lubricants against the manufacturer of Slick 50, a product which allegedly competes with the products sold by plaintiffs. The district court held that only "direct commercial competitors" or "surrogates" for direct commercial competitors have standing under § 43(a).[2] The Third Circuit affirmed the judgment, but invoked a different rationale. Specifically, the court determined that the critical question in such cases is whether the plaintiff has a reasonable interest to be protected from the false advertising. The court applied a test for addressing this issue which derives from the test for antitrust standing articulated by the Supreme Court in Associated Gen. Contractors of California, Inc. v. California State Council of Carpenters.[3] This test considers the following factors in a standing determination: "(1) the nature of the plaintiff's alleged injury; (2) the directness or indirectness of the asserted injury; (3) the proximity or remoteness of the party to the alleged injurious conduct; (4) the speculativeness of the damages claim; and (5) the risk of duplicative damages or complexity in apportioning damages."[4] Applying these factors to the facts at hand, the court determined that the plaintiff retail sellers lacked standing because they did not allege competitive harm and their damages could have been avoided by stocking the defendant's product. The court also recognized that allowing every party in the distribution chain to sue for false advertising would subject

---

[1] 165 F.3d 221, 49 U.S.P.Q.2d 1321 (3d Cir. 1998).

[2] Id. at 1323.

[3] 459 U.S. 519, 103 S.Ct. 897, 74 L.Ed.2d 723 (1983).

[4] Id. at 538–544 (*quoted in Conte Bros.*, supra, at 49 U.S.P.Q.2d at 1331).

defendants to multiple liability and the federal courts to needless litigation demands.

Add on page 117, as a second paragraph to Note 4:

In Lockheed Martin Corp. v. Network Solutions, Inc.,[5] a district court in California refused to extend the doctrine of contributory infringement to cover the relationship between NSI, the domain name registrar, and domain name registrants alleged to have directly infringed the plaintiff's mark. The court found that NSI's involvement with potentially infringing uses of domain names is remote,[6] and that NSI lacked unequivocal knowledge that a domain name was being used to infringe a trademark due to the "inherent uncertainty of trademark protection in domain names."[7]

Insert on page 117, after Note 4:

5. *Product Configurations*. Should the design of a race car be protected under trademark law? *Two Pesos* can be read as creating an expansive scope of protection under § 43(a). When this decision is coupled with the low standard for finding a likelihood of consumer confusion evinced in cases like *Lois Sportswear*, it can be argued that trademark law undermines the policies of patent law. In patent law, exclusive rights are provided only to inventors, only for very creative works, and only for a term of 20 years. In contrast, any distinctive designation can be protected under trademark law, even if not original to the trademark holder, and protection will endure for as long as the mark is used.

Some courts have responded to this concern by differentiating between product packaging and product configurations. Packaging usually has little functionality, and so these courts apply the *Two Pesos* analysis to them. Since configurations do often have functional dimensions, they apply "a more stringent test" ... in the product configuration context.[8] In Versa Products Company, Inc. v. Bifold Company (Manufacturing) Ltd.,[9] for example, Judge Becker had this to say about trade dress protection for directional control valves used in control panels of offshore oil-drilling rigs:

> First, the mere copying of product configurations does not suggest that the copier was necessarily trying to capitalize on the good will of the source of the original product. See Duraco [Products, Inc. v. Joy Plastic Enterprises, Ltd., 40 F.3d 1431 (3d Cir. 1994)], at 1453; see also infra at 205–08 (discussing implications of defendant's intent to copy). A presumption to the contrary would be mandated, if ever, only in the narrow class of cases where both (1) a product configuration is desirable to consumers primarily because of the configuration's inherent or

[5] 985 F.Supp. 949, 44 U.S.P.Q.2d 1865, 1875–1881 (C.D. Cal. 1997).

[6] Id. at 1877.

[7] Id. at 1881.

[8] Fun–Damental Too, Ltd. v. Gemmy Industries Corp., 111 F.3d 993, 1000, 42 U.S.P.Q.2d 1348, 1353 (2d Cir.1997).

[9] 50 F.3d 189 (3d Cir.), cert. denied, 516 U.S. 808, 116 S.Ct. 54, 133 L.Ed.2d 19 (1995).

acquired identification with the original source, and (2) the copier adopts affirmatively misleading labeling and/or marketing for the copied product, cf. Quaker Oats Co. v. General Mills, Inc., 134 F.2d 429, 432 (7th Cir.1943) ("The pirate flies the flag of the one he would loot. The free and honorable non-pirate flies the colors of his own distinctive ensign.").

Second, although a product's trade dress in the form of its configuration could function as an indicator of the product's source, product configurations in general are not reliable as source indicators, for functional configurations are not protected and thus may be freely copied, see Duraco, 40 F.3d at 1441, 1448–49, 1451, and inherently distinctive configurations will be rare, see id. at 1446. Since substantially identical products are often sold by different manufacturers under different names, consumers are accustomed to relying on product packaging and trademarks to identify product sources. Indeed, if any modification of the likelihood of confusion standard is justified in the product configuration context, the standard might well be heightened, perhaps to a "high probability of confusion."[10]

Some of these trade dress cases are also analyzed under a federal preemption doctrine, see Note 4 on page 138 of the main text and the insert into Note 8 of Assignment 25, infra in this Supplement.

PART B: NONCOMPETING GOODS

Add at page 134:

Ringling Bros.–Barnum & Bailey Combined Shows, Inc. v. Utah

United States Court of Appeals, Fourth Circuit, 1999.
170 F.3d 449.

■ PHILLIPS, Senior Circuit Judge:

This case requires us to interpret and apply the dauntingly elusive concept of trademark "dilution" as now embodied in the Federal Trademark Dilution Act of 1995 ("the Act"). See Federal Trademark Dilution Act of 1995, 15 U.S.C. §§ 1125, 1127. The concept was invoked in this case by Ringling Bros.-Barnum & Bailey Combined Shows, Inc. ("Ringling") in a claim under the Act that Ringling's "famous" circus trademarks slogan, THE GREATEST SHOW ON EARTH ("GREATEST SHOW mark"), had been diluted by the State of Utah's commercial use of its trademark slogan, THE GREATEST SNOW ON EARTH ("GREATEST SNOW mark"), as an advertisement of the state's winter sports attractions. The district court

---

[10] Id., at 201.

found that Ringling had not proved dilution under the Act and gave judgment for Utah. We affirm the judgment.

I

The relevant background facts as found by the district court are undisputed. From 1872 to the present, Ringling and its predecessors have offered their circus to the public as the "Greatest Show on Earth." In 1961, Ringling received federal trademark registration for its GREATEST SHOW mark for entertainment services in the nature of a circus.

Since its inception, Ringling has used its mark to advertise circus performances. The circus travels throughout the United States and presents approximately 1,000 shows annually to some 12 million people in 95 cities. More than 70 million people each year are exposed to the GREAT-EST SHOW mark in connection with the circus. Revenues derived from goods and services bearing or using the mark are substantial and exceeded $103 million for the fiscal year ending January, 1997.

Ringling advertises its circus using the GREATEST SHOW mark in print advertising, radio, television, videos, outdoor billboards, direct-mail pieces, press announcements, posters, program books, souvenirs, and joint promotions with other companies. In the fiscal year ending January 1997, expenditures on advertising using the mark totaled approximately $19 million. Through joint promotions with retailers, Ringling obtains significant additional exposure for its mark. Also, because of its renown, the GREATEST SHOW mark receives substantial free publicity.

Defendant Utah Division of Travel Development ("Utah") is an agency of the State of Utah. As early as 1962, Utah began using its GREATEST SNOW mark in connection with Utah tourism services. Utah has used its mark in magazine advertisements every year from 1962 to the present except 1963, 1977, and 1989. Utah has authorized the Utah Ski Association to use the GREATEST SNOW mark in connection with the Association's promotion of Utah tourism. Utah's primary use of its mark in Utah is its display on motor vehicle license plates. For each of the past fifteen years, Utah's budget for winter advertising, including advertising of the GREAT-EST SNOW mark, has ranged from $300,000 to $450,000.

In 1965, the Utah Attorney General opined that Utah's mark did not impair or violate Ringling's GREATEST SHOW mark. Utah registered its mark with the State of Utah in 1975 and renewed its registration in 1985 and 1995. In 1988, Utah applied to the United States Patent and Trademark Office to register its mark. Although Ringling opposed Utah's application, Utah was granted federal registration for its mark on January 21, 1997.

On June 6, 1996, Ringling commenced this action, seeking injunctive and monetary relief, on allegations that Utah's use of the GREATEST SNOW mark "diluted" Ringling's GREATEST SHOW mark in violation of the Act. Before trial, the district court granted Utah's motion to strike Ringling's demand for a jury trial, and after a bench trial, found for Utah.

This appeal by Ringling followed. Before us, Ringling challenges the district court's determination on the merits that Utah's mark did not dilute Ringling's mark in violation of the Act, and the court's denial of its demand for jury trial. We take these in turn.

II

The Federal Trademark Dilution Act, which became effective on January 16, 1996, amended Section 43 of the Lanham Act to provide a new cause of action for federal trademark "dilution." Under the Act, the owner of a "famous mark" is given protection "against another person's commercial use . . . of a mark or trade name, if such use begins after the mark has become famous and causes dilution of the distinctive quality of the mark." 15 U.S.C. § 1125(c)(1). A successful claimant may be given injunctive and, if a willful violation is proved, restitutionary, compensatory, and specific relief in the form of a destruction of offending articles. See id. §§ 1125(c)(1)-(2), 1117(a), 1118.

The Act defines dilution as:

> the lessening of the capacity of a famous mark to identify and distinguish goods or services, regardless of the presence or absence of—
>
> (1) competition between the owner of the famous mark and other parties, or
>
> (2) likelihood of confusion, mistake, or deception.

Id. § 1127.

And, the Act's legislative history further indicates that Congress understood that "dilution" might result either from "uses that blur the distinctiveness of [a famous] mark or [that] tarnish or disparage it." See H.R.Rep. No. 104–374, at 2 (1995), U.S. Code Cong. & Admin. News at 1029, 1029. The parties here both accept this as a proper reflection of congressional intent respecting the meaning of "dilution," and further agree that only dilution by blurring is at issue in this case.

To prove its statutory dilution claim, Ringling's burden therefore was to prove (1) that its mark was a "famous" one; (2) that Utah adopted its mark after Ringling's had become famous; and (3) that Utah's mark diluted Ringling's by "blurring" it. See id. §§ 1125(c)(1), 1127.

[The district court held for Utah]. Specifically, the court rejected Ringling's contention that proof alone of an "instinctive mental association" of the two marks by viewers sufficed to prove "dilution." While recognizing that to prove dilution by blurring one must necessarily prove as a threshold element a mental association by viewers of the marks themselves, the court held that this alone did not suffice. Rather, the court held, dilution by blurring occurs only where consumers "mistakenly associate or confuse the marks and the goods or services they seek to identify and distinguish,'' and this association causes actual harm to the senior mark's capacity to "identify and distinguish." Id. at 615–16. Applying this interpretation of "dilution" to Ringling's consumer survey evidence, the court found that the attempted proof by this means failed. See id. at 616–18. And, finally, analyzing the evidence as a whole under a multi-factor balancing test proposed for the purpose in Mead Data Central, Inc. v. Toyota Motor Sales, U.S.A., Inc., 875 F.2d 1026, 1035 (2d Cir.1989) (Sweet, J., concurring),[11] the court concluded that "dilution" had not been established on a balancing of those factors. See id. at 618–22.

A.

Ringling's primary challenge is to the district court's interpretation of the statutory meaning of "dilution," hence of the elements of the "dilution" claim newly created by the Act. As in the district court, it contends for its contrary interpretation: that a famous mark is "diluted" whenever a junior mark is sufficiently similar that consumers viewing them "instinctively make a mental association" of the two. It therefore argues that the district court erred in interpreting the Act to require further proof that in making this "mental association" consumers "mistakenly associate or confuse the marks and the goods or services they seek to identify and distinguish." And, it further argues that the court erred in interpreting the Act to require proof of "actual dilution."

Reviewing de novo the statutory interpretation issue, see Shafer v. Preston Memorial Hosp. Corp., 107 F.3d 274, 277 (4th Cir.1997), we disagree with Ringling's proffered "mental-association-alone" interpretation. Though we do not agree in every particular with the district court's interpretation, we agree with its basic points that "dilution" under the federal Act consists of (1) a sufficient similarity of marks to evoke in consumers a mental association of the two that (2) causes (3) actual harm to the senior marks' economic value as a product-identifying and advertising agent.

[handwritten margin note: ACCD'G TO DISTRICT CT: THE 3 THINGS YOU NEED TO CONSTITUTE DILUTION UNDER THE FEDERAL ACT]

That meaning surely does not leap fully and immediately from the statutory text. But, we believe it is the necessary meaning of the Act's critical provisions when read in light of the Act's legislative history. By that, we mean both the immediate but quite meager legislative record and, more critically, the broader background out of which the basic concept emerged and has evolved in state and federal trademark law. Though the process is laborious, we believe the historical inquiry has to begin far back with intellectual origins.

The concept of trademark "dilution" as distinct from "infringement" is commonly traced (though there were exploratory judicial antecedents) to

---

[11] [The Mead factors to determine the likelihood of confusion by blurring, as per Judge Sweet, are: 1) similarity of the marks; 2) similarity of the products covered by the marks; 3) sophistication of consumers; 4) predatory intent; 5) renown of the senior mark; 6) renown of the junior mark, see 875 F.2d at 1035.—eds.]

Frank I. Schechter. See Restatement (Third) of Unfair Competition '25 cmt. b. (1995) [hereinafter, Restatement]; see also Mead Data Central, 875 F.2d at 1028; Norm Thompson Outfitters, Inc. v. General Motors Corp., 448 F.2d 1293, 1299 (9th Cir.1971). Pointing up the inadequacies of then-current trademark law to serve its consumer-protection function in the complex, multi-layered marketing systems that had now evolved, Schechter first proposed simply expanding the protections provided by the consumer-protection model to accommodate the new market realities. See Frank I. Schechter, The Historical Foundations of the Law Relating to Trade–Marks (1925).

Two years later however, Schechter had concluded and advanced the thesis that the consumer-protection model, even in its expanded state, could not adequately accommodate the realities of twentieth century marketing. See Frank I. Schechter, The Rational Basis of Trademark Protection, 40 Harv. L. Rev. 813 (1927) [hereinafter Schechter, Rational Basis of Trademark Protection]. His proposal now was to abandon that model entirely, recognize that "the preservation of the uniqueness of a trademark . . . constitute[s] the only rational basis for its protection," id. at 831, and provide that protection by prohibiting "dilution" of such a mark's uniqueness from which it derived its hard-earned advertising value and selling power. See id. at 832 (borrowing the term "diluted" from a German case). Under that proposal, trademark law would have been confined to preventing the "dilution" of truly "unique" marks identified as those employing "coined, arbitrary or fanciful words or phrases that have . . . from the very beginning, been associated in the public mind with a particular product." Id. at 829. And, by "dilution" under this model was meant simply any junior use of an identical or sufficiently similar mark, without regard to whether the junior use had any other harmful effect than its necessary destruction of the senior mark's former absolute "uniqueness" as a product symbol. See id. at 825. This flowed from Schechter's thesis that the "real injury" caused by concurrent use of such marks was not consumer confusion but "the gradual whittling away or dispersion of the identity and hold upon the public mind of the mark or name by its use upon non-competing goods." Id. Protection of the public against deceptive and confusing uses of non-"unique" marks would have been left under such a regime to other laws than that of trademark.

This radical dilution proposal, whose practical effect if fully adopted would be to create as the whole of trademark-protection law property rights in gross in suitably "unique" marks, never has been legislatively adopted by any jurisdiction in anything approaching that extreme form. In fact, though from the outset its basic concept evoked occasional favorable judicial notices, see, e.g., Tiffany & Co. v. Tiffany Prods., Inc., 147 Misc. 679, 264 N.Y.S. 459, 462 (N.Y.Sup.Ct.), aff'd, 237 A.D. 801, 260 N.Y.S. 821 (1932), aff'd, 262 N.Y. 482, 188 N.E. 30 (1933), there was no legislative adoption of the concept in any form until 1947 when Massachusetts enacted the first state "antidilution" statute. See Act of May 2, 1947, ch.

307, § 7a, 1947 Mass. Acts 300 (codified as amended at Mass. Gen. Laws Ann. ch. 110B, § 12 (West 1996)). Over the next fifty years, other states followed suit and by 1996, when the President signed the federal Act into law, around half of the states had done so. See Restatement, supra § 25 statutory note. Though they of course varied in detail, the state statutes typically had four features of relevance for our interpretive purposes: (1) they defined the category of marks protected against dilution solely by reference to their "distinctive quality"; (2) they proscribed not just actual, consummated dilution, but the "likelihood of dilution"; (3) by containing no express reference to harm to the senior mark's economic value, they defined dilution in terms susceptible to the interpretation that it consisted solely of a loss of the mark's distinctiveness; and (4) they provided only injunctive relief. See, e.g., N.Y. Gen. Bus. Law § 360–1 (McKinney 1998); Ala.Code § 8–12–17 (1998); Cal. Bus. & Prof.Code § 14330 (West 1998).

It was against this background that Congress in 1995 brought the dilution concept into federal trademark law by the Federal Trademark Dilution Act's amendment of the Lanham Act. See 15 U.S.C. §§ 1125(c), 1127.[12] Though the sparse congressional record of the amendment's adoption contains no allusion to this background, its principal features must necessarily have figured in Congress's understanding and purpose in adopting the concept almost seventy years after it was first proposed in theoretical form and almost fifty years after the states had first brought it into state trademark law. That history, consisting of the concept as first proposed, the states' legislative adoption of modified forms, and the courts' reaction to the eventual state antidilution legislation, provided the sole primary sources for congressional understanding of the concept and purpose for adopting it in any form.

The most critical aspect of that history for our purposes is the experience of courts in interpreting and applying the state antidilution statutes. The broad outlines of that experience are fairly summarized by the Restatement on Unfair Competition in a comment to its section on "Dilution and Tarnishment":

> At first the courts applied the statutes reluctantly, if at all. In many cases dilution claims were denied because the plaintiff failed to prove a likelihood of confusion, notwithstanding the clear language of the statutes eliminating confusion as an element of the cause of action. Some courts, and numerous commentators, expressed fear that the uncertain limits of the antidilution cause of action would unduly expand the ability of trademark

---

[12] Two earlier unsuccessful attempts had been made to enact a federal dilution statute. The first was in 1932 with a bill advanced by Schechter. See H.R. 11592, 72d Cong. § 2(d)(3) (1932); Walter J. Derenberg, The Problem of Trademark Dilution and the Antidilution Statutes, 44 Cal. L. Rev. 439, 449 (1956) (quoting Schechter's testimony in hearings before the House Committee on Patents). The second attempt did not come until 1988, as a proposed amendment to the Lanham Act. See David S. Welkowitz, Reexamining Trademark Dilution, 44 Vand. L. Rev. 531, 537(1991) (discussing the fate of the 1988 bill).

owners to monopolize language and inhibit free competition. A broad antidilution theory also has the potential to render superfluous the traditional likelihood of confusion standard of liability. It was further suggested that a state cause of action for dilution might interfere with the federal policy of uniform, national trademark protection implemented under the Lanham Act, although only isolated cases supported this preemption theory. Other commentators, however, continued to urge protection for the selling power of well-known trademarks. After the New York Court of Appeals in Allied Maintenance Corp. v. Allied Mechanical Trades, Inc., 42 N.Y.2d 538, 399 N.Y.S.2d 628, 369 N.E.2d 1162 (1977), expressed the need for protection against the "cancer-like growth of dissimilar products or services which feeds upon the business reputation of an established distinctive trade-mark or name," judicial acceptance of the antidilution statutes increased. Nonetheless, in apparent recognition that broad interpretation of the statutes would undermine the balance between private and public rights reflected in the traditional limits of trademark protection, the courts have continued to confine the cause of action for dilution to cases in which the protectable interest is clear and the threat of interference is substantial.

Restatement, supra § 25 cmt. b.

Within that general experience, several features are of particular relevance to our purpose. First is the sheer difficulty that courts have had in getting a firm handle on the basic concept of "dilution" as cryptically expressed in the typical state statute in an unelaborated reference to "dilution of the distinctive quality of a mark." E.g., N.Y. Gen. Bus. Law § 360–1.

More important for our purposes than the continuing difficulty itself are its causes and its nature. And these plainly emerge in the cases. In the broadest sense, the cases demonstrate that once the dilution concept is sought to be given any form other than that of Schechter's simple original proposal it begins to lose its coherence as a legally enforceable norm. Specifically, it becomes difficult to identify the legal interest sought to be protected from "dilution," hence the legal harm sought to be prevented. As proposed by Schechter, the interest was easily identified as simply the mark's "uniqueness"—its singularity as a word-symbol contrived by its owner from outside "the human vocabulary"—and the harm, as a loss of that uniqueness. Schechter, Rational Basis of Trademark Protection, supra at 829. And, the legal cause of such a harm was the equally simple act of perfect or near-perfect replication of the senior mark by a junior mark. That all such "unique" marks had present or potential economic value— "selling power"—was assumed, as was the fact that any replication necessarily would "whittle away" that power. Id. at 830–31. Under that model, therefore, no proof would be required to prove dilution except the fact that a junior mark replicated the protected mark: no economic harm beyond that need be independently proved. See id. As commentators have fairly observed, the effect of this radical dilution model would have been to create property rights in gross in the narrow category of marks it protected, making them comparable (though without their time-limits) to those protected by patent and copyright law. See, e.g., Robert N. Klieger, Trademark Dilution: The Whittling Away of the Rational Basis for Trademark Protection, 58 U. Pitt. L. Rev. 789, 802 (1997) [hereinafter Klieger, Trademark Dilution].

Although when the state antidilution statutes began to be enacted the dilution concept had found expression as a legal construct only in the form proposed by Schechter, it is clear that none of the original or following statutes purported to enact that specific form. Instead, without defining the term, their typical formulation simply proscribed and made subject to injunction the use of any mark that created a "[l]ikelihood of . . . dilution of the distinctive quality of a [senior] mark . . . notwithstanding the absence of competition between the parties or of confusion as to the source of goods or services." Model State Trademark Act § 12 (1964), reprinted in, J. Thomas McCarthy,3 McCarthy on Trademarks and Unfair Competition § 22:8 (4th ed.1998) [hereinafter 3 McCarthy]. As earlier indicated, this bare-bones codification, centered on an unelaborated term of art having no previously acquired meaning through the common law decisional process, has puzzled courts from the outset as to just exactly what legal interest it sought to protect, and legal harm to prevent.

While perfectly synthesizing the courts' varying approaches to the interpretive problem is impossible, a few observations relevant to our interpretive purpose can be ventured. The first is that though the typical state statute formulation is susceptible to an in-gross-property-right interpretation—by reading "distinctive quality" as essentially synonymous with "uniqueness" in the Schechter model—no court seems to have taken that blunt approach. Instead, frequently alluding to Schechter's identification of the senior mark's "selling power," and the "whittling away" of that power as the ultimate concerns of dilution's special protective function, the courts seem generally to have assumed that loss of that power, and the economic value it represents, was the end harm at which the antidilution statutes were aimed.

The real interpretive problem has been with how harm to the senior mark's selling power resulting from the junior mark's use could be proved. Logic has compelled agreement that as a threshold matter some mental association of the two marks by a relevant universe of consumers must be proved (or presumed) in order to allow inference of the necessary causal connection between use and proven harm. And, plain statutory text has directed that the threshold mental association and any resulting harm need only be proved as matters of future "likelihood." But beyond these points of agreement the difficulty has remained: how, in the absence of any consumer confusion as to source, can harm to the senior mark's selling power traceable to the junior mark's use be proved even as likely future fact? On that, no consensus has emerged in judicial interpretations and applications of the state statutes. Three general approaches can be discerned in the efforts over time to deal with the problem.

[An extensive review of cases applying state dilution laws shows that after a period of "general judicial hostility to the whole statutory dilution concept"], the courts have either (1) assumed that its essential elements—mental association, causation, harm—could be found (or rejected) as fact by inference from a balancing of the "Mead factors," or (2) assumed that all those elements could be conclusively presumed—direct or inferential proof being impossible—simply from proof of the identity or near-identity of the two marks.

From all this, it is evident that the most significant feature of the state antidilution statutes has been their requirement that only a "likelihood of dilution" rather than actual dilution need be proved to entitle a claimant to the injunctive relief which they provide as the sole statutory remedy. This has enabled the courts to avoid hard definition of the economic harm to a senior mark's "selling power" that they generally agree is an essential element of statutory "dilution." And, even more critically, the necessary speculativeness of any inquiry into future states and conditions has led some courts to allow the essential elements of "likely" dilution to be inferred as fact from the "Mead factors," or, even more drastically, to be presumed from no more than the identity or sufficient similarity of the two marks.

We have explored the judicial experience with state antidilution statutes at this length because of the needed light it sheds upon the significance of key contrasting provisions of the federal Act. And, because of the light shed in turn by those provisions upon the specific interpretive issue we consider: whether, as Ringling essentially contends, "dilution" under the federal Act requires no more proof than sufficient similarity of junior mark to senior to evoke in consumers an "instinctive mental association" of the two.

Two key provisions of the federal Act, considered in relation to the state statutes and their interpretation bear directly upon that issue and provide its answer. Most critically, the federal Act proscribes and provides remedy only for actual, consummated dilution and not for the mere "likelihood of dilution" proscribed by the state statutes. And, by specifically defining dilution as "the lessening of the capacity of a famous mark to identify and distinguish goods or services," the federal Act makes plain what the state statutes arguably may not: that the end harm at which it is aimed is a mark's selling power, not its "distinctiveness" as such.

Accepting these two critical points, we therefore interpret the Act, in general agreement with the district court, as requiring for proof of "dilution" (1) a sufficient similarity between the junior and senior marks to evoke an "instinctive mental association" of the two by a relevant universe of consumers which (2) is the effective cause of (3) an actual lessening of the senior mark's selling power, expressed as "its capacity to identify and distinguish goods or services."

This concededly is a stringent interpretation of "dilution" under the federal Act. It confines the federal dilution claim to a more narrow scope than that generally now accorded by courts to state-law dilution claims. But, given the critical provisions that expressly differentiate the federal Act on key points from the state statutes, we must assume that this was exactly what was intended by Congress. It obviously is directly at odds with the mental-association-alone interpretation urged by Ringling, and Ringling challenges it in respects that require discussion.

Take first the property-right-in-gross interpretation. While Ringling does not press that interpretation in those exact terms, it is sufficiently implicit in its argument to require addressing. Doing so, we simply cannot believe that, as a general proposition, Congress could have intended, without making its intention to do so perfectly clear, to create property rights in gross, unlimited in time (via injunction), even in "famous" trademarks. Had that been the intention, it is one easily and simply expressed by merely proscribing use of any substantially replicating junior mark.

Neither can the Act be interpreted to require proof of actual economic harm and its effective cause but permit them to be judicially presumed from proof alone of the marks' sufficient similarity. As earlier noted, that process has been used by some courts in applying state antidilution statutes that require proof only of a "likelihood of dilution." Whatever may be the justification for using it in that setting, it could not properly be used under a statute requiring proof of actual harm already caused by use of a junior mark.

B.

We turn now to Ringling's challenges to the district court's determination that on the evidence adduced, Ringling had not proved dilution under the federal Act.

1.

It is important to remember that in keeping with its legal theory that it need prove only an "instinctive mental association" of the two marks, Ringling's survey was designed to develop only that fact. And, correspondingly, that in assessing the evidence under its quite different interpretation, the district court was looking for more: for actual harm to the senior mark's capacity to "identify and distinguish" resulting from any mental association of the marks evoked for consumers by the junior mark's use.

We begin our review of the district court's assessment of the survey evidence by summarizing the survey's methodology and results. The survey was conducted by interviewing individuals at seven shopping malls throughout the country, including one in Utah. At each location, randomly

LANHAM ACT
1125(c)

selected shoppers were presented with a card containing the fill-in-the-blank statement "THE GREATEST _____ ON EARTH" and were asked what word or words they would use to complete the phrase. If the shoppers completed the statement, they were asked with whom or what they associated the completed statement. And, they were asked further whether they could think of any other way to complete the statement, and with whom or what they associated the resulting statement.

The survey results showed that . . . in Utah (1) 25% of the respondents completed the statement THE GREATEST _____ ON EARTH with only the word "show" and associated the completed statement with the Circus; (2) 24% completed the statement with only the word "snow" and associated the completed statement with Utah; and (3)21% of respondents completed the statement with "show" and associated the result with the Circus and also completed the statement with "snow" and associated the completed statement with Utah. The survey further showed that outside of Utah (1) 41% of respondents completed the statement THE GREATEST _____ ON EARTH with only the word "show" and associated the completed statement with the Circus; (2) 0% completed the statement with only the word "snow" and associated the completed statement with Utah; and (3) fewer than 0.5% of respondents completed the statement with "show" and associated the result with the Circus and also completed the statement with "snow" and associated the completed statement with Utah. (Id. at 484.)

The district court concluded that this evidence failed to show dilution under the Act. In the first place, the court found the survey results inadequate to prove that consumers even made the requisite threshold mental association of the marks. When faced with the fill-in-the-blank phrase, "The Greatest _____ on Earth," some consumers filled in the blank with both the words "show" and "snow." When asked with whom or what they associated the completed phrase "the Greatest Show on Earth," virtually every consumer—inside Utah and outside Utah—indicated in one way or other that they only associated Ringling's circus with that phrase. When asked with whom or what they associated the completed phrase, "The Greatest Snow on Earth," every single consumer—inside Utah and outside Utah—indicated that they only associated Utah with the completed phrase. Not one consumer indicated that he associated the phrase, "The Greatest Show on Earth" with the phrase, "The Greatest Snow on Earth." Summarizing these results, the district court concluded that they were "strong evidence of the absence of dilution, not the presence of it," 955 F.Supp. at 617, that is, that they tended to disprove rather than to prove the required threshold mental association of the marks.

2.

[As to Ringling's contention that the district court wrongly assessed the so-called "Mead factors"] [w]e are persuaded, in agreement with other courts and commentators, and in probable agreement with some of the obvious discomfort of both parties in this case, that, by and large, the Mead-factor analysis simply is not appropriate for assessing a claim under the federal Act.

* * * * *

III

We turn finally to Ringling's challenge to the district court's order striking its demand for a jury trial. The district court first concluded that the Act did not provide a right to jury trial. See Ringling Bros.-Barnum & Bailey, Combined Shows, Inc. v. Utah Div. of Travel Dev., 955 F.Supp. 598, 599–601 (E.D.Va.1997). Turning to whether the Seventh Amendment, however, compels the right the court noted that except where a defendant "willfully intended . . . to cause dilution," the only remedy available to a dilution plaintiff is an injunction. See id. at 603 (quoting 15 U.S.C. § 1125(c)(2)). And, it then properly held that "where only an injunction is available to remedy dilution, the Seventh Amendment does not compel a jury trial." Id.; see generally 9 Charles Alan Wright & Arthur R. Miller, Federal Practice & Procedure § 2308 (2d ed.1994) ("[T]here is no constitutional right to a jury trial on a claim for an injunction."). And, then concluding that Utah was entitled to summary judgment on the issue of "willful intent," the district court ruled that because Ringling was therefore limited to injunctive relief on its dilution claim, it was not constitutionally entitled to a jury trial.

Add the following paragraph to Note 3a. (*Dilution*) on p. 136:

How responsive is the *Ringling Bros.* court to the trademark holder's interests in preventing deterioration and preserving cachet? Is the court right in thinking that a broad scope turns the trademark into a right in gross? Is this necessarily a bad thing? As noted earlier in the Supplement, dilution has proved an important way to protect domain name owners from those who use their trademarks as internet addresses. Will this right of action be as useful under this holding? Is such protection needed in light of the establishment of ICANN, see Supplement, supra?

Substitute the following paragraph for the last three paragraphs of Note 4 on pp. 139–140:

To what extent should states be permitted to protect marks against dilution in light of the federal dilution statute? For example, should states be permitted to protect against dilution a marketing device that is not famous enough to qualify for federal protection? Should Congress's decision to limit protection to famous marks preempt the states from acting in this area? Does the harsh eye cast by the *Ringling Bros.* court on the state-law cases suggest that, at the very least, state laws that turn on the *likelihood* of dilution are preempted?

Add the following after Note 5 on page 140:

6. *Dilution and marketing strategies.* The *Ringling Bros.* opinion was heavily edited for this Supplement. In another part of the decision, the court made the following argument for requiring more than mere proof of a mental association:

> It is not at all improbable that some junior uses will have no effect at all upon a senior mark's economic value, whether for lack of exposure, general consumer disinterest in both marks' products, or other reasons. Indeed, common sense suggests that an occasional replicating use might even enhance a senior mark's "magnetism"—by drawing renewed attention to it as a mark of unshakable eminence worthy of emulation by an unthreatening non-competitor. Imitation, that is, may occasionally operate in the marketplace as in social manners as the "sincerest form of flattery." In any event, there are enough reasons why replicating junior use of a mark might not cause any actual economic harm to a senior mark that it is not a proper subject for judicial presumption.[13]

In the section of the opinion dealing with what the survey evidence proved, the court continued this line of reasoning:

> And the [district] court found the survey results even more lacking as proof that Utah's use of its mark had caused any "lessening" of the "capacity" of Ringling's trademark slogan to "identify and distinguish" its circus as the mark's subject. Specifically, the court pointed to survey results indicating that consumer familiarity with Ringling's mark was greater in Utah (46%), where Utah's mark was well-known, than in the rest of the country (41%), where Utah's mark was virtually unknown, and that virtually every viewer questioned associated Ringling's mark (as distinguished from the fill-in-the-blank slogan) with, and only with, the Ringling circus and not "with Utah, with wintersports, or with any activities that are attributable to Utah's use of [its mark]."[14]

Isn't the Fourth Circuit correct in thinking that uses of a mark on noncompeting goods can enhance the effectiveness of the mark for all purposes? Look around: do the holders of important trademarks—Martha Stewart, Starbucks, Bill Blass—behave as though dilution is a problem? In a recent article, it was suggested that one reason why Levi Strauss, the blue jeans company, has suffered from decreasing sales is precisely that its mark isn't being used *enough*:

> Maybe one of Levi's problems is that it has no cola. It has no denim-toned house paint. Levi makes what is essentially a commodity: blue jeans. Its ads may evoke rugged outdoorsmanship, but Levi hasn't promoted any particular life style to sell other products. Once people

---

[13] 170 F.3d at 460.   [14] Id. at 463.

get to know a brand's most famous product, the thinking goes, they will trust that brand to deliver any number of items, even if the original product has no relationship to the subsequent stuff the company hawks. To wit: Brooks Brothers now has its own line of wines and Jack Daniel's sells clothes. "Great marketers say the brand can be the thing that holds their group of consumers together," said Sam I. Hill, a principal partner at Helios Consulting in New York. "The life-style label is an intelligent reaction by marketers who want a deeper relationship with consumers."[15]

[15] Jennifer Steinhauer , That's Not a Skim Latte. It's a Way of Life, New York Times, March 21, 1999, at Sec. 4, p. 5, col. 1.

ASSIGNMENT 4

THE INTEREST IN PUBLIC ACCESS

PART A: TRADEMARKS AS LANGUAGE

Add on page 171 the following paragraph after the first paragraph of Note 5:

In Mattel Inc. v. MCA Records, Inc.,[1] the manufacturer of the Barbie doll and the owner of "Barbie" marks was denied a preliminary injunction in a trademark infringement and dilution action against the writers, producers and singers of the song "Barbie Girl". Relying on the standard in *New Kids*, the court concluded that the defendants might have a viable defense to the trademark infringement action since the defendants' work was a parody of Barbie's "party-girl" image shared by at least some members of the public. The court also found that Mattel was not likely to succeed in proving consumer confusion between its line of Barbie dolls and the *Barbie Girl* song. Finally, with respect to the dilution claim, the court concluded that the defendants' use of "Barbie" probably should be exempt as a noncommercial use, but even if this is not the case, the First Amendment concerns still require a balancing of principles in a case such as this.

Substitute the following paragraph for Note 7 on page 174:

7. *Functionality.* Recall that at the registration stage, genericity and functionality were treated similarly. Just as certain words were considered too important to communication to be made anyone's exclusive property, certain shapes were considered too utilitarian to be registered. Until 1998, cancellation of a registration was permitted at any time for a mark that had become generic, but not necessarily for a mark that was deemed functional. To reverse this anomaly, § 1064(3) of the Lanham Act was amended in 1998 to provide that if at any time a registered mark is functional, a cancellation petition can be filed by anyone who believes that he is or will be damaged by the registration. Thus, functionality now is treated the same as genericity from the standpoint of both registration and cancellation.

---

[1] 46 U.S.P.Q.2d 1407 (C.D. Cal. 1998).

ASSIGNMENT 5

REMEDIES

1. INTRODUCTION

Add on page 192 before the first full paragraph:

Recently, several courts have held the Trademark Remedy Clarification Act ("TRCA"), which abrogated the states' Eleventh Amendment immunity, unconstitutional in light of the Supreme Court's decision in Seminole Tribe of Fla. v. Florida.[1] In *Seminole*, the Supreme Court affirmed section five of the Fourteenth Amendment as the only basis upon which Congress can abrogate the states' immunity under the Eleventh Amendment. Since the congressional enforcement power under the Fourteenth Amendment is not unlimited, courts have required the TRCA to further the goals of protecting property from state action taken without due process of law. Thus, the focus of the litigation adjudicating the constitutionality of the TRCA has been on whether it protects a property right recognized under the Fourteenth Amendment. In College Savings Bank v. Florida Prepaid Postsecondary Education Expense Board,[2] the Third Circuit held the TRCA unconstitutional as applied in that case because the only right which was involved there was the right to be free of false advertising under § 43(a), which the court did not believe was an intangible property right protected under the Fourteenth Amendment. As this Supplement was in the process of being printed, the Supreme Court issued an opinion affirming the Third Circuit's ruling, holding that the TRCA does not permit a State to be sued for its alleged misrepresentation of its own product.[3] The Court's reasoning in this opinion can, in one sense, be construed fairly narrowly in that it largely seems to turn on the notion that the nature of the plaintiff's interests in this case is not "property" within the meaning of the Fourteenth Amendment. Also, it is arguable that the Court is suggesting that its holding is only applicable to § 43(a) actions. Still, on the same day this opinion was issued, the Court also concluded that the Patent Remedy Clarification Act ("PRCA") was an unconstitutional exercise of Congress' authority because, although patents clearly are property for purposes of the Fourteenth Amendment, the PRCA is not justified as appropriate remedial

---

[1] 517 U.S. 44, 116 S.Ct. 1114, 134 L.Ed.2d 252 (1996).

[2] 131 F.3d 353, 45 U.S.P.Q.2d 1001 (3d Cir. 1997).

[3] College Savings Bank v. Florida Prepaid Postsecondary Education Expense Board, ___ U.S. ___, 119 S.Ct. 2219, ___ L.Ed.2d ___ (1999).

legislation designed to remedy a Fourteenth Amendment violation.[4] *See infra* in this Supplement in Assignments 13 & 24. In a third opinion issued the same day, the Court held in an action brought against the state of Maine for violating the Fair Labor Standards Act, that Congress could not subject a state to suit in state court absent the state's consent.[5] Taken together, these new rulings potentially indicate a tremendous, and very worrisome, shift in the federal/state balance regarding lawsuits against states.

Add at the end of Note 9 on page 231:

In 1996, Congress passed the Anti–Counterfeiting Consumer Protection Act.[6] This statute increases the criminal and civil penalties for the counterfeiting of copyrighted and trademarked products and makes available statutory damages to plaintiff trademark owners for losses attributable to trademark counterfeiting. The range of statutory damages is between $500 and $100,000 per counterfeit mark for each type of goods or services, and if the defendant's conduct was willful, statutory damages can be awarded up to $1,000,000 per counterfeit mark.

[4] Florida Prepaid Postsecondary Education Expense Board v. College Savings Bank, ___ U.S. ___, 119 S.Ct. 2199, ___ L.Ed.2d ___ (1999).

[5] Alden v. Maine, ___ U.S. ___, 119 S.Ct. 2240, ___ L.Ed.2d ___ (1999).

[6] P.L. 104–153; 110 Stat. 1386.

COPYRIGHT PROTECTION: INTRODUCTION

Insert on page 234 immediately after the text accompanying footnote 6:

In 1998, President Clinton signed into law the "Sonny Bono Copyright Term Extension Act", which extends the copyright term for an additional twenty years. Copyright protection now generally lasts for the life of the author plus seventy years.

ASSIGNMENT 7

THE REQUIREMENTS OF ORIGINALITY AND AUTHORSHIP

3. MATERIALS FOR SOLUTION OF PRINCIPAL PROBLEM

Add to the end of Note 3 on p. 284:

Recently, two courts have disagreed about the scope of protection West has in its case arrangements. In Oasis Publishing Co. v. West Publishing Co.,[1] a federal district court in Minnesota held that West's arrangement of its cases, including the internal pagination, is an original work of authorship entitled to copyright protection. The Second Circuit disagreed with this conclusion in Matthew Bender & Co. v. West Publishing Co.[2] In that case, the court affirmed a summary judgment for Matthew Bender and held that West's star pagination's volume and page numbers are unprotected information. Moreover, the court rejected West's argument that the plaintiffs' compilations of judicial opinions stored on their CD–ROM discs which embed West's star pagination is a "copy" of West's copyrighted arrangement within the meaning of § 101's definition of "copies". West argued that its copyright arrangement is duplicated by the plaintiffs because their discs, which contain the star pagination, permit a user to manipulate the data embedded on the disc and to retrieve the cases in the order in which they appear in West's case reporters. Therefore, West argued that the plaintiffs' discs are copies because West's copyrighted arrangement is "fixed" on the discs in a way that can be "perceived ... with the aid of a machine of device." The Second Circuit concluded, however, that "[t]he natural reading of the statute is that the arrangement of the work is the one that can be perceived by a machine without an uninvited manipulation of the data."[3] Additionally, the Second Circuit issued a companion opinion affirming a decision following a bench trial which allowed Hyberlaw to scan cases in West Reporters (excluding the headnotes), thus rejecting West's argument that it has a protectible copyright interest in the decisions deriving from its various editorial steps.[4]

[1] 924 F. Supp. 918 (D. Minn. 1996).

[2] 158 F.3d 693, 48 U.S.P.Q.2d 1545 (2d Cir. 1998).

[3] Id. at 1553.

[4] Matthew Bender & Co. v. West Publishing Co., 158 F.3d 674, 48 U.S.P.Q.2d 1560 (2d Cir. 1998).

Add after the first paragraph of Note 5 on page 285:

In Entertainment Research Group, Inc. v. Genesis Creative Group, Inc.,[5] the Ninth Circuit also adopted a higher standard of originality for derivative works. That case involved three-dimensional inflatable costumes based upon the cartoon characters whose copyrights were owned by the companies purchasing the costumes. In discussing whether these costumes are copyrightable as derivative works, the court distinguished derivative works based on underlying works in the public domain and those such as were involved in this case where the derivative work is based on a preexisting copyrighted work. The court noted that "[t]his difference is critical because in deciding whether to grant copyright protection to a derivative work, courts must be concerned about the impact such a derivative copyright will have on the copyright privileges and rights of the owner of the underlying work."[6] Applying the originality test for derivative works adopted by the Second Circuit in Durham Industries, Inc. v. Tomy Corp.,[7] see the Copyright Office regulation reprinted in the casebook, the court determined that any differences existing between the costumes and the underlying two-dimensional copyrighted characters were attributable to functional considerations, and therefore could not support the originality of the costumes.[8] Also, the court was concerned that granting Entertainment Research Group a copyright on the costumes would afford them a "de facto monopoly on all inflatable costumes depicting the copyrighted characters" also in their costumes.[9] See also the Principal Problem in Assignment 8.

[5] 122 F.3d 1211 (9th Cir. 1997).

[6] Id. at 1219.

[7] 630 F.2d 905, 909 (2d Cir. 1980).

[8] Id. at 1223.

[9] Id. at 1224.

ASSIGNMENT 8

SUBJECT MATTER: USEFUL ARTICLES AND PROTECTION FOR CHARACTERS

Insert the following at the end of Note 5 on page 316:

In *Leicester v. Warner Brothers*,[1] a federal district court in California concluded that by enacting § 120(a), Congress intended to substitute the new protection afforded architectural works "for the previous protection sometimes provided under the conceptual separability test for non-utilitarian sculptures (such as gargoyles and stained glass windows) incorporated into a work of architecture."[2] The court also noted that under its interpretation of the statute, conceptual separability would be limited to situations which do not involve architectural works.

Insert the following Note after Note 5 on page 316:

6. *Protection for Vessel Hulls.* As part of the Digital Millennium Copyright Act, which was signed into law in October, 1998, Congress created a new form of protection for the design of vessel hulls by adding chapter 13 to the copyright statute.[3] Although protection under this provision is limited to vessel hulls no longer than 200 feet,[4] some observers believe that this new protection might be used as a model for more widespread design protection sometime in the future. Chapter 13 provides for a ten year term of protection, which begins upon the earlier of the "date of publication of the registration . . . or the date the design is first made public."[5] If registration "for the design is not made within two years after the date on which the design is first made public," the protection under this chapter is lost.[6] Infringement under this chapter includes making or importing for sale or for use in trade any infringing article; and the selling or distributing for sale or for use in trade any infringing information.[7] The chapter provides for a variety of remedies including injunctive relief; damages; infringer's profits; and attorney's fees.[8] The chapter expires on October 28, 2000, two

[1] 47 U.S.P.Q.2d 1501 (C.D. Cal. 1998).
[2] Id. at 1508.
[3] 17 U.S.C. § 1301 et. seq.
[4] 17 U.S.C. § 1301(b)(3).
[5] 17 U.S.C. §§ 1304; 1305(a).
[6] 17 U.S.C. § 1310 (a).
[7] 17 U.S.C. § 1309(a).
[8] 17 U.S.C. §§ 1322 & 1323.

years from the date of its enactment; during the period in which it is in effect, the Copyright Office must conduct two joint studies with the Patent and Trademark Office regarding the impact of this chapter.

7.   *The New Hague Agreement.* In 1925, the Hague Agreement Concerning the International Deposit of Industrial Designs was completed by WIPO. The treaty intended to establish a process for obtaining protection of industrial designs at an international level. The treaty was revised in 1934 and again in 1960, and currently has 29 signatories. The United States did not join the earlier versions of the Hague Agreement because many of its provisions were inconsistent with U.S. law.

In 1991, an expert committee began to revise the Hague Agreement in order to remove the barriers that prevented nations such as the United States from joining the agreement. The New Hague Agreement establishes a central filing system administered by WIPO for foreign design protection. The entire process for acquiring this protection would be streamlined and made less expensive to industrial design owners. A diplomatic conference to finalize the Draft Treaty is scheduled to meet during the summer of 1999 in Geneva, Switzerland.

Under the New Hague Agreement, WIPO determines whether an international application meets all minimum requirements, assigns the filing date, registers the application and forwards the application to the parties involved. WIPO then publishes the international registration and the signatories have a limited time to decide whether to register or grant protection to the industrial design. The term of protection is 15 years from the date of registration of the industrial design.

Under the new treaty, an applicant can file one English-language application with the PTO and will receive protection in all signatories to the New Hague Agreement. Currently, owners wishing to protect their industrial designs must file an application in each of the individual states where their designs are utilized. Implementation of this treaty in the U.S. would be through design patent law.

ASSIGNMENT 9

THE RECIPIENTS OF COPYRIGHT'S INCENTIVES: OWNERSHIP, THE WORK FOR HIRE DOCTRINE, RENEWAL AND TERMINATION RIGHTS, AND MORAL RIGHTS

Insert prior to the Introduction on page 318:

The effect of the "Sonny Bono Copyright Term Extension Act" extending the copyright term for an additional twenty years not only impacts the length of copyright protection generally, but also the length of protection for works made for hire and joint works. For works made for hire, the copyright now lasts for a term of ninety-five years from the year of the work's first publication, or a term of one hundred and twenty years from the year of its creation, whichever expires first (see § 302(c)). In the case of joint works, the period of protection lasts for seventy years after the death of the last surviving author's death (see § 302(b)).

Insert as the last paragraph of Note 1 on page 357:

The Second Circuit subsequently applied the joint authorship test announced in *Childress* in an interesting suit by a dramaturg against the playwright of the critically acclaimed Broadway musical *Rent*. In *Thomson v. Larson*,[1] the court interpreted the intention standard announced in *Childress* to mean more than a consideration of the parties' words or their "professed state of mind." Instead, *Childress* "suggested a more nuanced inquiry into factual indicia of ownership and authorship, such as how a collaborator regarded herself in relation to the work in terms of billing and credit, decisionmaking, and the right to enter into contracts."[2] After evaluating this evidence, the Second Circuit affirmed the district court's judgment that the dramaturg was not a joint author.

Thomson v. Larson also raised the interesting question as to whether the dramaturg could retain the copyright in her contribution to the play even if the court finds that the mutual intent requirement for joint

[1] 147 F.3d 195, 47 U.S.P.Q.2d 1065 (2d Cir. 1998).

[2] Id. at 1070.

30

authorship is lacking. Since the dramaturg raised this issue for the first time on appeal to the Second Circuit, however, the court refused to decide this matter. Note that this issue also is raised in the Principal Problem.

Read the following in conjunction with Note 3 on page 357:

Again, as a result of the Sonny Bono Copyright Term Extension Act, copyright protection now lasts for a single term consisting of the life of the author plus seventy years (see § 302(a)). The Sonny Bono Act did not, however, impact upon the time frame in which the termination provisions can be exercised.

Insert the following in conjunction with the first full paragraph of Note 4 on page 359:

One effect of the Sonny Bono Copyright Term Extension Act is the lengthening of the renewal extension by twenty years. Thus, § 304(a) now provides that the copyright is automatically extended for a 67–year renewal period at the end of the original 28–year term.

Also, a new subsection (d) was added to § 304 which provides that for copyrights already in their renewal terms at the effective date of the Sonny Bono Copyright Term Extension Act, the termination right still can be exercised by appropriate persons if the termination right period has already expired. This amendment allows for termination during a period of 5 years beginning at the end of 75 years from the date the copyright originally was secured as long as the author or owner of the termination right has not previously exercised the termination right. Works made for hire are, of course, expressly exempted from this provision.

THE SCOPE OF THE COPYRIGHT HOLDER'S RIGHTS: INFRINGEMENT

Add on page 407 after the second paragraph in Note 5:

In Computer Associates International Inc. v. Altai, Inc.,[1] the Second Circuit held that *res judicata* and collateral estoppel do not bar the plaintiff's action for copyright infringement in France despite the U.S. ruling that OSCAR 3.5 does not violate the plaintiff's United States copyright. The court reached this conclusion regarding *res judicata* because the defendants' infringing conduct, which was the basis of the French action, occurred after the plaintiff had filed the lawsuit in the United States, and also because the New York district court lacked jurisdiction over one of the French defendants. With respect to the collateral estoppel issue, the court reasoned that Altai failed to show the copyright standards in France and the United States are sufficiently "identical" for purposes of applying that doctrine.

Add on page 408 at the end of Note 5:

Title III of the Digital Millennium Copyright Act (see Note 11 below) amended § 117 of the 1976 Copyright Act to provide that "it is not an infringement for the owner or lessee of a machine to make or authorize the making of a copy of a computer program if such copy is made solely by virtue of the activation of a machine that lawfully contains an authorized copy of the computer program, for purposes only of maintenance or repair of that machine" as long as the new copy is not used in any other manner and is destroyed immediately after the maintenance or repair is finished. Thus, Congress has reversed the Ninth Circuit's decision in *MAI Systems.*

Insert on page 410 after Note 10:

11. *The Digital Millennium Copyright Act.* On October 28, 1998, President Clinton signed this extensive amendment to the 1976 Copyright Act (the "DMCA") into law. The DMCA implements the following two 1996 World Intellectual Property Organization treaties: the WIPO Copyright Treaty and the WIPO Performances and Phonograms Treaty. Of the five titles composing the DMCA, Titles I and III are most directly related to the

---

[1] 126 F.3d 365, 44 U.S.P.Q.2d 1281 (2d Cir. 1997).

themes explored in this Assignment. Title III is treated above as part of Note 5. Title I treats new technology and therefore essentially is not directly related to the traditional copyright infringement doctrines. Still, a brief discussion of this Title is warranted and probably fits best overall in the discussion of copyright infringement generally.

Title I, the *WIPO Copyright Performances and Phonograms Treaties Implementation Act of 1998*, amends the 1976 Copyright Act in part by adding Chapter 12. This new chapter deals generally with a) the circumvention of technological measures invoked by copyright owners as protective steps; and b) tampering with copyright management information.

The new § 1201 distinguishes between technological measures preventing unauthorized access to a copyrighted work and those preventing unauthorized copying of a copyrighted work. Regarding those measures preventing unauthorized access, the statute prohibits both certain circumventional conduct as well as circumventional devices. Regarding those measures preventing unauthorized copying, only certain circumventional devices are prohibited. The statute was drafted to allow circumventional conduct with respect to measures preventing unauthorized copying to enable the public to continue to make a fair use of copyrighted works. The prohibition against circumventing conduct regarding measures preventing unauthorized access does not become effective until October, 2000, because the Copyright Office wants time to study whether there are classes of works that present a particular danger of public exclusion. In addition, certain types of circumvention are permitted with respect to the following six categories: nonprofit library, archive and educational institutions;[2] reverse engineering;[3] encryption research;[4] protection of minors;[5] personal privacy;[6] and security testing.[7]

Prohibited devices include those which are primarily designed to circumvent; those with a limited commercially significant purpose other than to circumvent; and those which are knowingly marketed for uses in circumventing. Circumvention is defined in § 1201(a)(3)(A) as descrambling a scrambled work; decrypting an encrypted work; or otherwise avoiding, bypassing, removing, deactivating, or impairing a technological measure without the authority of the copyright owner.

Section 1202 treats maintaining the integrity of copyright management information. Section 1202(a) prohibits the knowing provision or distribution of false copyright management information if done "knowingly and with the intent to induce, enable, facilitate, or conceal infringement."

[2] § 1201(d).
[3] § 1201(f).
[4] § 1201(g).
[5] § 1201(h).
[6] § 1201(I).
[7] § 1201(j).

Section 1202(b) prohibits the intentional removal or alteration of copyright management information, and the distribution of such altered works.

The remedies for violating Chapter 12 essentially comport with those for other copyright infringements. Section 1203 provides for an array of equitable and monetary relief. With respect to innocent infringers, courts have discretion to reduce or remit damages under § 1203(c)(5). Section 1204 specifies criminal sanctions.

ASSIGNMENT 12

THE FAIR USE DOCTRINE AND OTHER PUBLIC ACCESS CONSIDERATIONS

PART A: THE FAIR USE DOCTRINE

Add the following at the end of Note 10 on page 492:

Relying on the theory of *Lasercomb,* the Fifth Circuit in Alcatel USA Inc. v. DGI Technologies, Inc.,[1] concluded that a plaintiff's licensing agreement for its operating system software for telephone routing equipment constitutes copyright misuse because it enabled the plaintiff to use its copyrights to gain indirect commercial control over its non-copyrighted microprocessor cards.

Add the following after Note 10:

11. *Vicarious Liability and the Digital Millennium Copyright Act.* The *Sony* opinion explores vicarious liability and contributory infringement in the context of copyright law. Title II of the DMCA adds a new section 512 to the Copyright Act[2] which addresses vicarious liability for copyright infringement for online service providers. This new provision provides limitations on liability based for the following four categories of conduct by a service provider: 1) transitory communications—when providers merely act as data conduits by transmitting digital information from one point on a network to another at the request of a third party; 2) system caching— when providers, for a limited time period, store copies of material that has been made available online by someone other than the provider, and then transmitted to a subscriber at his or her direction; 3) when providers host systems with infringing materials, provided service providers do not have actual knowledge of the infringement and act immediately to remove the infringing material; and 4) when providers link users to a site containing infringing material by using information location tools such as hyperlinks, online directories and search engines (this fourth limitation is subject to

---

[1] 166 F.3d 772, 49 U.S.P.Q. 2d 1641 (5th Cir. 1999).

[2] Note that the Fairness in Musical Licensing Act also added a new § 512 to the Copyright Act (see Note 2 *infra* in Part B, Public Access Considerations). This duplication of statutory section numbers will need to be corrected in a subsequent amendments bill.

the same types of conditions as the third limitation). All four limitations completely bar monetary damages and provide restrictions on the availability of injunctive relief. This new provision also includes a section governing the limitation of liability for nonprofit educational institutions.

12. Soon after the publication of the original casebook, the Sixth Circuit issued a significant and controversial *en banc* fair use opinion involving photocopying of coursepacks containing copyrighted material, Princeton University Press v. Michigan Document Services, Inc.,[3] and subsequently, the Supreme Court denied *cert.*[4] Initially, the district court had held that a copyshop's practice of failing to obtain permission for the photocopying of excerpts on a fee-per-page of copyrighted materials for inclusion in coursepacks sold to students was not fair use. The district court also awarded damages that may have been enhanced for willfulness.[5] A three-judge panel of the sixth circuit then reversed this ruling.[6] In the *en banc* opinion, the Sixth Circuit affirmed the district court's ruling as to liability but concluded that the district court erred in its finding of willfulness. The *en banc* 8–5 ruling therefore vacated the district court's damage award on the ground that it may have been linked to its finding of willfulness. The Supreme Court's denial of *cert.* leaves the *en banc* opinion as the final word in this case.

The *en banc* opinion performed a typical fair use factor based analysis. In analyzing what it deemed as the most critical factor, "the effect of the use upon the potential market for or value of the copyrighted work," the court reiterated a presumption derived from *Sony* that in a case of noncommercial use, the copyright holder must sustain the burden of proof as to market effect, while in the case of a commercial use, the defendant maintains this burden. Here, the court ruled that the defendant's use was commercial even though the ultimate users were students, since the copyshop's failure to obtain permission gave it a competitive edge over other copyshops that did pay royalties. Even if the challenged use was noncommercial, however, the court felt that the publishers met their burden of proving that the copyshop's practice diminished the potential market value of their works since the publishers of the works in question were collecting permission fees in an amount of almost $500,000 per year. As to the remaining fair use factors, the court deemed them "considerably less important" in a case such as this, where the use is nontransformative.[7] The court held that the purpose and character of the use factor weighed against fair use in this case since the use was commercial. Also weighing against fair use was the expressive nature of the publishers' works in question, as well as the amount and substantiality of the defendant's use of the publishers' works. Additionally, the court considered the "Classroom

[3] 99 F.3d 1381 (6th Cir.1996).

[4] 520 U.S. 1156, 117 S.Ct. 1336, 137 L.Ed.2d 495 (1997).

[5] 855 F.Supp. 905 (E.D.Mich.1994).

[6] 74 F.3d 1512 (6th Cir.1996).

[7] 99 F.3d at 1388.

Guidelines" before Congress in enacting the fair use provision, and observed that the defendant's use was "light years away from the safe harbor" of these guidelines.[8] The court also concluded that from a policy standpoint, the publishers require incentives to continue their activities even if the authors themselves would continue to write scholarly pieces absent these incentives. Finally, the court concluded that in light of the controversy sparked by the litigation's history, the copyshop's belief that its conduct amounted to fair use was not so unreasonable as to constitute willfulness for purposes of determining the appropriate statutory damages.

There were three separate dissents, the longest of which claimed that the majority erred by 1) focusing on the loss of permission fees in its market effect analysis; 2) finding that evidence exists supporting the view that permission fees provide an important incentive for publishers; and 3) invoking legislative history, particularly the "Classroom Guidelines."[9] This dissent found that the use in question is no different from that of a student who chooses to make a photocopy of the excerpts in question. Although the use in question is not transformative, this dissent dismissed the relevance of this aspect of the first fair use inquiry given the educational use of the materials. Moreover, this dissent disputed the commercial aspect of the use because it claimed that the appropriate use is that by the students rather than the mechanical reproduction by the copyshop. In light of the noncommercial use, this dissent relied on the presumption of no harm to the publishers' market. As to the second fair use factor, this dissent simply noted the expressive nature of the works in question and stated that this factor "does little more than confirm that the works at issue are protected by copyright and may only be used 'fairly' ".[10] Regarding the third factor, the dissent stated that the record lacked evidence that the excerpts were so substantial that the coursepacks "superseded the original works or otherwise exceeded the proper educational purposes that could justify the reproduction."[11] Regarding the fourth factor, market impact, this dissent emphasized what he believed was the circularity of the majority's reasoning in finding that market harm exists based on the loss of permission fees precisely because the publishers are alleging a right to the permission fees. In the dissent's view, no market harm exists because the defendant's practice did not impair the value of either the original works themselves or a derivative product of those works which the copyright holder seeks to market. This dissent also questioned the majority's reliance on the Classroom Guidelines in light of the lack of ambiguity in the statute itself.

Think about the following questions based on *Princeton University Press* as they pertain to the fair use discussion in this chapter. 1) Is this case different from that of a professor who distributes copies of a copyrighted work to her class on the ground that the copyshops are in business and

---

[8] Id. at 1391.

[9] 99 F.3d at 1398.

[10] Id. at 1405.

[11] Id. at 1407.

were able to get a competitive edge over those copyshops that did pay royalties? 2) Whose use is relevant in assessing whether the case involved commercial use—that of the copyshops or the use by the students? 3) Regarding the market impact analysis, *Sony* seemed to ignore that the copyright owner has the right to exploit any and all potential markets for the copyrighted work. Yet, if there is a market for permission fees, who should have a right to it? 4) Does *Acuff-Rose* make transformative use critical for all types of cases, or just those involving parody?

The following Part B substitutes for Assignment 11 in the casebook.

PART B: PUBLIC ACCESS CONSIDERATIONS

1. INTRODUCTION

In the original edition of this casebook, we had a separate chapter on *The Interest in Public Access*. Recent amendments to the copyright statute have, however, largely eliminated the need to treat much of this material with the Problem and case approach invoked throughout the rest of the casebook. Therefore, the issues relevant to the topic of Access will be addressed through a series of informational Notes, followed by Bibliographical References.

As discussed in Assignment 10, copyright law embodies the concept of ownership by enabling the copyright proprietor to exercise exclusively certain rights with respect to the protected work. In certain situations, however, copyright law recognizes the need to sanction unauthorized uses of copyrighted property. One of the most important such exemptions is the fair use doctrine, which is the subject of Part A of this Assignment. In addition to the fair use doctrine, the 1976 Copyright Act details a series of exempted activities that do not constitute copyright infringement and a series of limitations upon the scope of exclusive rights to copyrighted works. These exemptions and limitations are codified at Sections 107–120. Although many of these statutory sections are rather technical and complex, they must be read carefully to appreciate fully the delicate balance struck by copyright law between the interests of creators and the public in the copyrighted work. The following Notes highlight several topics including the most prominent of the statutory limitations involving public performance; the first sale doctrine; the Record Rental Amendment Act and the Computer Software Rental Amendments Act; public display; sound recordings; and compulsory licensing.

NOTES

1. *Public Performance.* The copyright owner's exclusive right to publicly perform her work is codified in § 106(4) of the statute. To fully explore the exemptions related to public performances, it is worth spending a moment considering what a public performance is. This is defined by § 101 of the statute, which provides that "[t]o perform or display a work 'publicly' means (1) to perform or display it at a place open to the public or at any place where a substantial number of persons outside of a normal circle of a family and its social acquaintances is gathered; or (2) to transmit or otherwise communicate a performance or display of the work to a place specified by clause (1) or to the public, by means of any device or process, whether the members of the public capable of receiving the performance or display receive it in the same place or in separate places and at the same time or at different times."[12] The first clause of this definition has been called the "public place" clause and the second clause, the "transmit" clause.[13]

In Columbia Pictures Industries, Inc. v. Redd Horne, Inc.,[14] the Third Circuit considered the defendant's operation of two stores in which videos were rented for in-store viewing in private booths. When the door to the private viewing room was closed, a signal in the counter area at the front of the stores was activated and one of the store's employees placed the selected cassette into a video machine in the front of the store and the picture was transmitted to the patron's private booth. The court ruled that the defendant's stores qualified as a "public place" under the first clause of the statutory definition because the stores were "open to the public." Therefore, the court did not have to consider whether the place of performance involved the gathering of "a substantial number of persons outside of a normal circle of a family and its social acquaintances." According to the court, the "relevant 'place' within the meaning of section 101['s definition of public performance] is each of Maxwell's two stores, not each individual booth within each store". Moreover, although the court relied on the "public place" clause rationale, it bolstered its conclusion by looking to the "transmit" clause contained in the statutory definition of public performance and the accompanying legislative history indicating that the transmission of a performance to members of the public can occur even if the people are in private settings and are viewing the performances at different times.

In Columbia Pictures Industries v. Professional Real Estate Investors,[15] the court affirmed a grant of summary judgment in favor of the defendant hotel in a copyright infringement suit by movie companies

---

[12] § 101 (1991).

[13] See Columbia Pictures Industries, Inc. v. Professional Real Estate Investors, Inc., 866 F.2d 278 (9th Cir. 1987)

[14] 749 F.2d 154 (9th Cir. 1984).

[15] 866 F.2d 278 (9th Cir. 1987).

against the defendant based on the hotel's practice of providing videodiscs for rent to its guests for viewing in their rooms. Can a meaningful distinction be made between the hotel rooms in *Professional Real Estate* and the viewing booths in *Redd Horne* for purposes of applying the "public place" clause of the statutory definition of public performance? What if the booths in *Redd Horne* contained equipment which allowed the patrons to operate the video cassettes themselves, rather than having to rely on an employee of the store to start the video? Is a prison more like a hotel room or like the situation in *Redd Horne*? What factors should be considered in determining the status of prisons? What other institutions raise a similar set of issues?

2. *Section 110(5) and the Fairness in Music Licensing Act.* The purpose of § 110(5) is to exempt from copyright infringement liability anyone who simply turns on, in a public place, an ordinary radio or television. Until 1998, this section exempted from infringement the communication of a "transmission embodying a performance or display of work by the public reception of the transmission on a single receiving apparatus *of a kind commonly used in private homes*...." (emphasis supplied). Thus, proprietors of small commercial establishments who brought standard equipment onto their premises were exempt from liability. The legislative history to § 110(5) specified the following factors to consider in applying this exemption: "[T]he size, physical arrangement, and noise level of the areas within the establishment where the transmissions are made audible or visible, and the extent to which the receiving apparatus is altered or augmented for the purpose of improving the aural or visual quality of the performance for individual members of the public using those areas."[16] However, despite the guidelines provided by the statute, courts took different approaches both with respect to what factors should be considered, and how the relevant factors should be applied.[17]

[16] H.R. Rep. No. 94–1476, 94th Cong.2d Sess. 87 (1976), reprinted in 1976 U.S. Code Cong. & Admin. News 5659, 5701 (1977).

[17] Cases finding an exception under § 110(5) include Broadcast Music, Inc. v. Claire's Boutiques, Inc., 949 F.2d 1482 (7th Cir. 1991)(exemption found for company with more than 700 retail stores, each using two speakers hung from the ceiling, concealed speaker wire, and a receiver typically located in a closet or storage area); Edison Brothers Stores, Inc. v. Broadcast Music, Inc., 954 F.2d 1419 (8th Cir.), cert. denied, 504 U.S. 930, 112 S.Ct. 1995, 118 L.Ed.2d 590 (1992)(holding that § 110(5) exempts large chain of clothing stores where each store had 2 speakers that were not recessed and were placed within 15 feet of the receiver). Cases failing to find an exemption include: Cass County Music Co. v. Muedini, 55 F.3d 263 (7th Cir. 1995)(holding that § 110(5) did not apply to a restaurant using system with single receiver since it employed separate control panel with five selector switches, nine recessed speakers, and configuration allowing up to 40 speakers); Blue Seas Music, Inc. v. Fitness Surveys, Inc., 831 F.Supp. 863 (N.D. Ga. 1993)(no § 110(5) exemption where fitness facility had 13 recessed ceiling speakers and several floor speakers); Prophet Music, Inc. v. Shamla Oil Co., 26 U.S.P.Q.2d (BNA) 1554 (D. Minn. 1993)(no § 110(5) exemption for defendant's "music-on-hold" telephone system which used a receiving apparatus that was connected to sophisticated amplification and telecommunications equipment designed to retransmit the broadcasts over an unlimit-

In 1998, Congress enacted the Fairness in Music Licensing Act which defines the parameters of the "home-style" exemption in greater detail. Essentially, the statute exempts from liability public performances of nondramatic musical works originated by a licensed radio or television station in bars and restaurants having less than 3750 square feet; other establishments are exempt if they have less than 2000 square feet. For an establishment with a greater gross square footage than these specified amounts, the exemptions are as follows: audio performances are exempt if there are no more than six total loudspeakers, of which not more than four are in any one room; audiovisual performances are exempt if the visual portion is displayed by not more than four total devices, of which only one is located in any single room and has a diagonal screen no greater than 55 inches.

3. *ASCAP AND BMI.* One may question how the holders of copyrights in musical compositions insure that their rights are not violated. ASCAP (American Society of Composers, Authors, and Publishers) and BMI (Broadcast Music, Inc.) illustrate the principle that there is strength in numbers. The idea underlying these organizations is that a centralized body is better able to represent the interests of its individual members with respect to recouping royalty fees for public performances of music.[18] Taken together, ASCAP and BMI control ninety-five percent of the United States market for performance rights to musical compositions. ASCAP represents more than 40,000 composers and publishers and controls a repertoire of about 3 million compositions and BMI represents more than 100,000 members and controls about 1.5 million compositions.[19]

ASCAP and BMI are vigilant about protecting their members' interests. In this regard, consider the following article by Mike Royko, which is reprinted in the casebook on page 439 with the permission of the Chicago

---

ed number of callers' telephones); Red Cloud Music Co. v. Schneegarten, Inc., 27 U.S.P.Q.2d (BNA) 1319 (C.D. Cal. 1992)(no § 110(5) exemption for a restaurant using 8 ceiling recessed speakers with concealed wiring where the receiver/amplifier was located in a separate room and the restaurant was about 3,000 square feet); and U.S. Songs, Inc. v. Downside Lenox, Inc., 771 F. Supp. 1220 (N.D. Ga. 1991)(§ 110(5) did not apply to establishment containing 20 ceiling mounted speakers attached to a radio receiver placed behind a bar because the system was not of a type commonly used in private homes and the sounds were further transmitted since they were dispersed throughout the establishment).

[18] These organizations license only "nondramatic" or small performing rights, as op-

posed to "dramatic" or grand rights. Dramatic rights typically are licensed by agents who act in the interest of the copyright proprietors. See Scorese, Performing Broadway Music: The Demon Grand Rights Traps, 13 Colum.–VLA J.L. & Arts 261, 267 (1989).

[19] See Avery, The Struggle Over Performing Rights to Music: BMI and ASCAP vs. Cable Television, 14 Hastings Comm. & Ent L.J. 47, 51 (1991). The Copyright Clearance Center, which was established in 1977, performs essentially the same function as ASCAP and BMI in the context of photocopying copyrighted materials that are registered with the Center. The Center, as agent for publishers, grants blanket advance permission to photocopy the registered materials for a fee and remits these fees to the copyright owners.

Sun Times. Additionally, the Fairness in Musical Licensing Act discussed in Note 2 added a new section 512 to the Copyright Act which addresses the determination of reasonable license rates charged by performing rights societies.

4. *The scope of § 110.* The following hypotheticals are intended to illustrate the scope of some of the other exemptions in § 110.

a) Suppose a college student, in order to satisfy the requirements for a theater arts course she is taking, performs a number of songs sung by Madonna as part of a presentation about the singer. Is this copyright infringement?

b) Is it copyright infringement for your client to sing "Bridge Over Troubled Waters" at a Saturday night rock mass?

c) Suppose you hire a woman to entertain your daughter's friends at her 6th birthday party. The woman sings copyrighted songs, plays them on her guitar, and charges $100 for her services. Is this copyright infringement? Does it make a difference if the entertainer donates the money to UNICEF? Does it make a difference if the birthday girl's mom does the entertaining instead?

d) Is it copyright infringement for a shop that sells both exercise apparel and records to blast an audio cassette of the soundtrack of the movie "Flashdance" from speakers outside of the store?

5. *The first sale doctrine.* This doctrine has spawned several interesting issues which are explored below.

a. *The "core" first sale concept.* The first sale doctrine, which is codified at § 109(a), provides that notwithstanding the distribution right guaranteed by § 106(3), "the owner of a particular copy or phonorecord lawfully made under this title, or any person authorized by such owner, is entitled, without the authority of the copyright owner, to sell or otherwise dispose of the possession of that copy or phonorecord."[20] Thus, once a lawfully made copy of a copyrighted work is sold, the copyright holder has no control over subsequent sales or dispositions of that particular copy. What policies do you suppose support this doctrine?

Since the first sale doctrine only applies to copies of a copyrighted work, some have argued that it is becoming rapidly obsolete in an environment in which the contents of copyrighted works are being disseminated more frequently through electronic means such as the Information Superhighway.[21] The Digital Millenium Copyright Act of 1998 requires the Register of Copyrights and the Assistant Secretary of Commerce for Com-

---

[20] § 109(a).

[21] See Litman, The Exclusive Right to Read, 13 Card. Arts & Ent. L.J. 29 (1994); Litman, Copyright and Information Policy, 55 Law & Contemp. Probs. 185, 188–89, 208 (1992)(recommending the development of new alternatives such as "compulsory licenses for secondary uses of electronically disseminated works" to effectuate more complete access to copyrighted works).

munications and Information to commission a study of the impact of Title I of the Act (see Note 11 under Assignment 10 of this Supplement) on both the first sale doctrine and § 117 (allowing owners of computer programs a limited right to reproduce, see Note 5b *infra*). See also Note 5b below on the controversy regarding downloading music off the Internet.

b. *The Record Rental Amendment Act and the Computer Software Rental Amendments Act as exemptions to the first sale doctrine.* Section 109(b) embodies the Record Rental Amendment Act of 1984, and the Computer Software Amendments Act of 1990. The Record Rental Amendment Act was passed to interfere with the practice of record shops encouraging unauthorized recordings of copyrighted music by renting records and selling blank cassette tapes. As such, it is an exception to the first sale doctrine because it restricts the use and disposition of individual phonorecords by precluding the rental, lease, or lending of such works for direct or indirect commercial advantage. What is the scope of this prohibition?

Despite the enactment of the Record Rental Amendment Act, home taping still is prevalent because people simply use other sources rather than rely on rentals from commercial outlets. As you saw in Part A, making a home recording of a television show is a fair use. See Sony Corp. of America v. Universal City Studios, Inc.,[22] Should the same be true of home tapings of phonorecords?[23]

In 1992, Congress enacted the Audio Home Recording Act,[24] which requires the inclusion of the Serial Copy Management System (SCMS) in digital audio tape recorders (DATs). DATs are superior to compact discs (CD's) because they contain both a recording and a playback medium, and they allow a recording to be made which rivals that of CD's in terms of tonal quality. As one commentator has observed, "[i]f DAT were introduced in its present form any CD, itself a perfect copy of the original sound carrier, would become a master from which additional perfect copies could be made in every home with a DAT recorder."[25] The SCMS allows DATs to make direct, digital-to-digital copies of CD's and other pre-recorded cassettes, but precludes digital-to-digital copies of these copies. In other words, the Act sanctions an unlimited number of first-generation digital-to-digital copies of music, but outlaws second-generation copies of these works. Thus, this Act forges an interesting compromise respecting the appropriate degree of public access to phonorecords, CD's, and other objects in which sounds

---

[22] 464 U.S. 417, 104 S.Ct. 774, 78 L.Ed.2d 574 (1984).

[23] See generally Nimmer, Copyright Liability for Audio Home Recording: Dispelling the "Betamax" Myth, 68 Va. L. Rev. 1505, 1534 (1982)(observing that "audio home recording of copyrighted works has never been protected by any special exemption, express or implied, from the scope of the copyright laws" and is "not defensible under the 'fair

use' doctrine"; advocates the imposition of royalty payments on the sales of recording equipment).

[24] §§ 1001–1010.

[25] Horowitz, The Record Rental Amendment of 1984: A Case Study in the Effort to Adapt Copyright Law to New Technology, 12 Colum.–VLA J.L. & Arts 31, 68–70 (1987).

are fixed. The Act also requires a royalty payment of 3 percent of the transfer price on any digital audio recording medium imported, distributed or manufactured in the United States.[26] A digital audio recording medium is defined to exclude a material object embodying a sound recording when it is first distributed.[27] Thus, this royalty essentially applies to blank tapes. In addition, a 2 percent royalty is required on the importation, manufacture, and distribution in the United States of every digital audio recording device.[28] The Librarian of Congress arranges the distribution of royalties to the interested copyright parties.

Of course, the current controversy involves the downloading of music off the Internet. The bane of the recording industry's existence is MP3, a free technology for delivering music on line. This technology does not prevent the illegal copying of music and has thus become a vehicle for widespread music piracy on the Internet. Moreover, Real Networks, a leading manufacturer of Internet audio software, recently announced plans to launch a system designed to allow consumers to copy, store and play audio CD's on personal computers. This system also is designed to facilitate the playing of music transmitted by the Internet and can record and play music in several technical formats, including MP3. To combat such efforts, the Recording Industry Association of America has assembled a group known as the Secure Digital Music Initiative which seeks agreement on a standard for portable devices playing digital music. Impatient with its failure to promulgate such a standard, major record companies such as Universal Music are forging ahead with their own plans for digital distribution.[29] Days before this Supplement was submitted for publication, the Ninth Circuit held that a portable music player called the Rio, which allows users to download MP3 audio files from a computer and listen to them elsewhere, is not a digital audio recording device subject to the restrictions of the Audio Home Recording Act.[30] The basis for the decision was that the Rio cannot reproduce a digital music recording, either directly or indirectly from a transmission, and therefore does not qualify as a digital audio recording device under the Act.

Subsequent to the Record Rental Amendment Act, the Copyright Act was amended to provide yet another exemption to the first sale doctrine. Pursuant to the Computer Software Rental Amendments Act of 1990, the renting of computer software without the permission of the copyright owner for purposes of "direct or indirect commercial advantage" constitutes copyright infringement. See § 109(b). The objective of this amend-

[26] § 1004(b).

[27] § 1001(4)(B).

[28] § 1004(a).

[29] See John Markoff, "New System For PC Music Stirs Concern Over Piracy," New York Times, Sec. C, Page 1 (May 3, 1999); Matt Richtel, "Record Label to Distribute Music on Line," New York Times, Sec. C, Page 1 (May 3, 1999).

[30] Recording Industry Association of America v. Diamond Multimedia Systems, ___ F.3d ___, 1999 WL 387265 (9th Cir. 1999).

ment is similar to that of the Record Rental Amendment Act of 1984, to bolster the rights of copyright proprietors by making unauthorized home duplication more difficult, thus fostering sales of the protected work. Why should commercial rentals of records and computer software be treated differently from videos? What exceptions are provided by the Computer Software Rental Amendments Act of 1990? The copyrights of owners of computer programs also are limited by § 117 of the statute which allows the owner of a copy of a computer program to make another copy of the program if such copy "is created as an essential step in the utilization of the computer program in conjunction with a machine and . . . is used in no other manner" or "is for archival purposes only."

Discussion question. Should the exemptions from the first sale doctrine provided in § 109(b) be extended to library books? Specifically, should authors be compensated from public funds when their works are lent from libraries? This type of system is called a public lending right and it is operational in about twelve countries. How would such a system fare in this country?

c. *First sale and unauthorized importation.* What is the significance of the phrase "lawfully made under this title"?[31] In a recent decision resolving a conflict in the federal circuit courts, the United States Supreme Court held that Copyright Act does not bar the unauthorized importation of goods into the United States. In Quality King Distributors, Inc. v. L'anza Research International, Inc.,[32] a California manufacturer of hair care products unsuccessfully challenged the ability of a foreign company to import the domestically produced products back into the United States for resale at discount prices to unauthorized retailers. The domestic manufacturer, L'anza, sued a foreign distributor that had bought the goods abroad from one of L'anza's authorized foreign distributors. Affixed to the goods were copyrighted labels.

Section 602(a) provides that the unauthorized importation of copies that have been acquired outside the United States infringes the copyright owner's exclusive right to distribute under § 106. The question before the Court, then, was whether the first sale doctrine applies to imported copies sold abroad. The Supreme Court held that it does apply and reversed the lower courts. The District Court had entered summary judgment for plaintiff L'anza, and this ruling was affirmed by the Ninth Circuit.[33] The Supreme Court granted the petition for certiorari in light of the conflict

---

[31] The legislative history states that defendants should bear the burden of proving whether a particular copy was lawfully made or acquired. See H.R. Rep. No. 94–1476, 94th Cong., 2d Sess. 80–81, *reprinted in* 1976 U.S. CODE CONG. & AD. NEWS 5659, 5694–95.

[32] 523 U.S. 135, 118 S.Ct. 1125, 140 L.Ed.2d 254 (1998).

[33] L'Anza Research Intern., Inc. v. Quality King Distributors, Inc., 98 F.3d 1109, 1114 (9th Cir. 1996).

between the Ninth Circuit's opinion and that of the Third Circuit in Sebastian Int'l, Inc. v. Consumer Contacts Ltd.[34]

The language of § 602(a) provides that unauthorized importation is a violation of the copyright owner's exclusive right to distribute. In an opinion written by Justice Stevens, the Court noted that a copyright owner's exclusive right to distribute is qualified by the first sale doctrine. Since the exclusive right to distribute does not encompass resales by lawful owners that come within the scope of the first sale doctrine, both domestic and foreign owners of L'anza products who import and then resell them in the United States do not violate the importation provision.[35] In rejecting L'anza's argument that § 602(a) is superfluous if limited by the first sale doctrine, the Court emphasized that § 602(a) is in fact broader than § 109(a) because the former also encompasses copies that are lawfully made in another country and therefore not subject to § 109(a).[36] Moreover, the Court concluded that even though § 501(a) of the Copyright Act defines an infringer by referring separately to violations of sections 106 and 602, the other provisions of the statute compel the conclusion that § 602(a) does not function independently of the first sale doctrine.[37] Most significantly, because § 106 is subject not only to § 109(a) but also to §§ 107 to 120, the fair use defense codified in § 107 would also be unavailable to importers if § 602(a) were construed as a separate right not subject to the other statutory limitations. The Court found this interpretation untenable, particularly in light of the importance of the fair use defense and the unlikely event that Congress intended to ban completely all imports containing any copyrighted material protected by a United States copyright.[38]

The Court noted that this copyright case was unusual because L'anza was primarily interested in protecting the integrity of its marketing method rather protecting its right to prevent unauthorized reproduction of copyrighted labels.[39] However, the Court affirmed that its legal interpretation of the Copyright Act would apply as well to cases involving more traditional copyrighted subject matter such as books and sound recordings.[40] Although *L'anza* apparently resolves the application of the first sale doctrine and the importation prohibition in the context of domestically manufactured goods, the Supreme Court has yet to resolve definitely situations where the copies sought to be imported were produced abroad, and thus were not made "under this title" within the meaning of § 109(a). See Assignment 5.

---

[34] 847 F.2d 1093 (3d Cir. 1988)(holding that the manufacturer and copyright owner of domestically manufactured goods with copyrighted labels that were sold to foreign distributors and then imported into this country without the copyright owner's permission was precluded by the first sale doctrine from establishing infringement based on the unauthorized importation).

[35] 118 S.Ct. at 1130.

[36] Id. at 1131.

[37] Id. at 1132.

[38] Id. at 1133.

[39] Id. at 1128.

[40] Id.

6. *Display*. Section 109(c) of the Copyright Act provides another limitation on a copyright owner's exclusive rights. That subsection states that the owner of a lawfully made copy of a copyrighted work can publicly display that copy, without the copyright owner's permission, "either directly or by the projection of no more than one image at a time, to viewers present at the place where the copy is located."[41] Does this provision strike a reasonable balance between the competing interests of copyright owners and copy owners?

Some commentators also have advocated the adoption of a right of private display for visual artists which would become operative upon the resale of the work.[42] Functionally, this right is equivalent to a resale royalty provision, which also is known as *droit de suite*. Under *droit de suite*, visual artists have a right to a percentage of the resale sales price of their works. Currently, California is the only state with such a statute,[43] and the Register of Copyrights has recommended against the adoption of resale royalties at this time.[44]

7. *Sound recordings and digital sampling*. Pursuant to TRIPS, it is now unlawful for anyone to, without the consent of the performer involved, fix the sounds or sounds and images of a live musical performance. It is also unlawful to reproduce, transmit, or distribute a copy or phonorecord of such a performance from an unauthorized fixation. Section 101 makes anyone who does these prohibited activities subject to the civil remedies for copyright infringement, and criminal sanctions for such actions can be invoked pursuant to 18 U.S.C. § 2319A. These measures give musicians added protection from unauthorized fixation and trafficking in their performances.

Section 114 of the Copyright Act defines the scope of exclusive rights in sound recordings. Note that the statutory definition of sound recordings provides that they "are works that result from the fixation of a series of musical, spoken, or other sounds ... regardless of the nature of the material objects, such as disks, tapes, or other phonorecords, in which they are embodied."[45] Section 114 of the statute states that the exclusive rights of the owner of a copyright in a sound recording are limited to the rights of reproduction, distribution, and preparation of derivative works under § 106, but do not include the exclusive rights to display the work and to perform it publicly (except for performances of sound recordings by means

---

[41] § 109(c).

[42] See Goetzl & Sutton, Copyright and the Visual Artist's Display Right: A New Doctrinal Analysis, 9 Colum.–VLA J.L. & Arts 15, 50, 53 (1984)(advocating the adoption of a compulsory license to effectuate this private right of display).

[43] Cal. Civ. Code § 986 (West Supp. 1993).

[44] Copyright Office Report Executive Summary, Droit de Suite: The Artist's Resale Royalty, 16 Colum.–VLA J.L. & Arts 381 (1992).

[45] § 101.

of a digital audio transmission under § 106(6) discussed below). Why does the statute makes this distinction?

In 1995, Congress enacted the Digital Performance Right in Sound Recordings Act which provides that copyright protection in sound recordings extends to performing "the copyrighted work publicly by means of a digital audio transmission" (§ 106(6)). The Act defines a "digital transmission" as "a transmission in whole or in part in a digital or other non-analog format."[46] It also contains exemptions for certain transmissions and re-transmissions,[47] as well as provisions for compulsory licensing.[48] The Digital Millennium Copyright Act further expands the relevant exemptions in connection with ephemeral recordings under § 112 of the Copyright Act to permit the making of a single ephemeral recording to facilitate the digital transmission of a sound recording permitted under the Digital Performance Right in Sound Recordings Act.

Section 114 also provides that with respect to the rights of reproduction and preparation of derivative works, the copyright owner has the exclusive right to duplicate the recording in forms that directly or indirectly recapture "the actual sounds fixed in the recording", but her rights "do not extend to the making or duplication of another sound recording that consists entirely of an independent fixation of other sounds, even though such sounds imitate or simulate those in the copyrighted sound recording."[49]

Why does the statute adopt this "actual reproduction" standard for infringement for sound recordings, thereby differentiating sound recordings from other types of copyrighted works that are infringed when the unauthorized reproduction or derivative work is "substantially similar"? Is the need for public access greater with respect to sound recordings than for other types of copyrighted works?

In light of the foregoing, consider the legality of digital sampling. Digital sampling is a technique that involves the following steps: the recordation of a sound, its analysis, decomposition, storage of the tonal qualities in a computer, possible electronic alteration, and playback. According to one commentator: "Digital sound sampling has been used as a technique to isolate distinctive vocal and instrumental sounds. Once isolated, these sounds may be recorded and analyzed. In fact, the process allows the digital sampler to create a new song. The digital sampler can then play back a song comprised of another artist's sounds but never actually executed by the original musician."[50] The use of digital sampling in the music industry is extremely prevalent, in terms of sampling both live performances as well as sound recordings. Still, its legality has been

---

[46] See § 101.
[47] See § 114(d).
[48] See §§ 114(d) & 115.
[49] § 114.

[50] Houle, "Digital Audio Sampling, Copyright Law and The American Music Industry: Piracy or Just a Bad 'Rap' ", 37 Loy. L. Rev. 879, 880 (1992).

specifically addressed by only a few courts.[51] What copyright issues are necessary to resolve in determining the legality of digital sampling?

8. *Compulsory licensing.* The Copyright statute contains several provisions for compulsory licensing. Section 111(c) provides for compulsory licenses for secondary transmissions by cable systems; § 112 encompasses a license for making ephemeral recordings (this licensing provision was added by the Digital Millennium Copyright Act); § 114 covers digital subscription transmissions of sound recordings (pursuant to the Digital Performance Right in Sound Recordings Act); § 115 mandates compulsory licenses for making and distributing phonorecords and licenses for digital phonorecord deliveries; § 116 provides for compulsory licenses for jukeboxes; § 118 specifies compulsory licenses for public broadcasters; and § 119 requires compulsory licenses for satellite retransmissions to the public for private home viewing. In addition, the Digital Millennium Copyright Act added to § 114 a provision expanding the license for digital subscription transmissions to include webcasting as a new category of "eligible nonsubscription transmissions." Webcasting refers to the use of the Internet to make a digital transmission of a sound recording with streaming audio technology.

The rates and terms of a compulsory license are determined in one of two ways, either through a process based upon voluntary negotiations,[52] or where necessary, by means of an arbitration proceeding as prescribed in Chapter 8 of the Copyright Act. Until 1993, the Copyright Royalty Tribunal ("CRT") was responsible for adjusting the rates and terms for the compulsory licenses and determining the distribution of those royalty fees collected pursuant to the Copyright Act. However, in 1993, Congress abolished the CRT with the passage of the Copyright Tribunal Reform Act of 1993, and vested authority for administering these proceedings in the Librarian of Congress.

What effect do compulsory licenses have on the price the copyright holder obtains for the work? What are the policies favoring and disfavoring compulsory licenses?

BIBLIOGRAPHY

The following is a sampling of some of the pertinent literature on the topics covered in the foregoing problem and materials:

[51] See Tin Pan Apple, Inc. v. Miller Brewing Co., 30 U.S.P.Q.2d 1791 (1994)("It is common ground that if defendants did sample plaintiff's copyrighted sound recordings, they infringed that copyright, whatever may be said of the composition copyright."); Jarvis v. A & M Records, 827 F. Supp. 282 (D.N.J. 1993)(denying defendants' motion for summary judgment in a copyright infringement action involving digital sampling); Grand Upright Music Ltd. v. Warner Bros. Records Inc., 780 F. Supp. 182 (S.D.N.Y. 1991)(indicating that unauthorized digital sampling violates the copyright law).

[52] See, e.g., 17 U.S.C. §§ 111(d)(4)(A); 112(e)(3)(4)(6) & (7); 114 (e) & (f); 115 (c)(3)(B)–(F); 116 (b); 118 (b)–(d)(2); 119 (c)(2). Many of these statutory provisions clarify that parties may enter into private agreements without raising antitrust concerns.

McKuin, Home Audio Taping of Copyrighted Works and the Audio Home Recording Act of 1992: A Critical Analysis, 16 Hastings Comm. & Ent. L.J. 311 (1994); The Computer Software Rental Amendments Act of 1990: The Nonprofit Library Lending Exemption to the "Rental Right", 41 J. Copyright Soc'y 231 (1994); Cochran, Why Can't I Watch This Video Here?: Copyright Confusion and Performances of Videocassettes & Video-discs in Libraries, 15 Hastings Comm. & Ent L.J. 837 (1993); Jensen, Is the Library Without Walls on a Collision Course with the 1976 Copyright Act?, 85 Law Lib. J. 619 (1993); Jehoram, The Neighboring Rights of Performing Artists, Phonogram Producers and Broadcasting Organizations, 15 Colum./VLA J.L. & Arts 75 (1990); Kernochan, The Distribution Right in the United States of America: Review and Reflections, 42 Vand. L. Rev. 1407 (1989); Scorese, Performing Broadway Music: The Demon Grand Rights Traps, 13 Colum.-VLA J. L. & A. 261 (1989); Horowitz, The Record Rental Amendment of 1984: A Case Study in the Effort to Adapt Copyright Law to New Technology, 12 Colum.–VLA J.L. & Arts 31 (1987); Korman & Koenigsberg, Performing Rights in Music and Performing Rights Societies, 33 J. Copyright Soc'y 332 (1987); Nevins, Antenna Dilemma: The Exemption from Copyright Liability for Public Performance Using Technology Common in the Home, 11 Colum.–VLA J.L. & Arts 403 (1987); Shipley, Copyright Law and Your Neighborhood Bar and Grill: Recent Developments in Performances and the Section 110(5) Exemption, 29 Ariz. L. Rev. 475 (1987); Kernochan, Music Performing Rights Organizations in the United States of America: Special Characteristics, Restraints, and Public Attitudes, 10 Colum.-VLA J.L. & Arts 333 (1986); Colby, The First Sale Doctrine: The Defense That Never Was?, 32 J. Copyright Soc'y 77 (1984); D'Onofrio, In Support of Performance Rights in Sound Recordings, 29 UCLA L. Rev. 168 (1981); Korman, Performance Rights in Music Under Sections 110 and 118 of the 1976 Copyright Act, 22 N.Y.L. Sch. L. Rev. 521 (1977).

ASSIGNMENT 13

REMEDIES

Add after the first paragraph on page 494:

In 1997, Congress passed the No Electronic Theft Act.[1] This statute provides criminal penalties for willful copyright infringement through electronic and other avenues. Specifically, it defines criminal infringement as either 1) infringement "for purposes of commercial advantage or private financial gain" or 2) "the reproduction or distribution, including by electronic means, during any 180–day period of 1 or more copies or phonorecords of 1 or more copyrighted works", with a total retail value of more than $1000. In 1998, Congress amended the definition of criminal infringement in § 506(a) to comport with the No Electronic Theft Act.

Add the following question to the middle paragraph of Note 1 on p. 514:

How does the majority's determination of the willfulness issue in *Princeton University Press* (discussed in the Supplement in Assignment 12) bear on the question of damages in the Principal Problem?

Add on page 514 as the last paragraph of Note 1:

In Feltner, Jr. v. Columbia Pictures Television, Inc.,[2] the United States Supreme Court held that § 504(c) of the statute does not, in and of itself, grant a defendant the right to a jury assessment of statutory damages, thus interpreting the word "court" as used in this provision to mean" judge" rather than "jury." Nonetheless, the Court went on to conclude that the right to a jury trial regarding statutory damages is mandated by the Seventh Amendment because a monetary remedy is legal in nature and not rendered equitable simply because such relief is not fixed or readily calculable. Perhaps the most interesting aspect of this opinion is Justice Scalia's concurrence on the ground that the statute itself should be interpreted to require a jury trial. In so concluding, Justice Scalia, a staunch proponent of the "textualist" school of statutory interpretation, resorts to legislative history to bolster his interpretation of the statute!

Add to Note 3 on page 517 before the first full paragraph:

The litigation holding the Trademark Remedy Clarification Act unconstitutional in light of Seminole Tribe of Fla. v. Florida,[3] see the discussion

---

[1] Pub. L. No. 105–147; 111 Stat. 2678.

[2] 523 U.S. 340, 118 S.Ct. 1279, 140 L.Ed.2d 438 (1998).

[3] 517 U.S. 44, 116 S.Ct. 1114, 134 L.Ed.2d 252 (1996).

in this Supplement under Assignment 5, has been paralleled in the context of the Copyright Remedy Clarification Act ("CRCA"). Seminole held that Congress did not act pursuant to a valid exercise of power when it abrogated state sovereign immunity by passing a law pursuant to the Indian Commerce Clause, a clause of Article I of the Constitution.[4] In Chavez v. Arte Publico Press,[5] the Fifth Circuit held that although copyrights are a species of property, section 5 of the Fourteenth Amendment does not embrace congressionally required waivers of state sovereign immunity in legislation such as the copyright law which is authorized by Article I constitutional powers. In other words, since Article I predates the Eleventh Amendment, it is not an appropriate basis upon which to supersede the Eleventh Amendment, which is a later amendment to the same document. The same result was reached by a district court in Rodriguez v. Texas Commission on the Arts.[6] As this Supplement was going to press, the Supreme Court held that the Patent Remedy Clarification Act ("PRCA") was an unconstitutional exercise of Congress' authority because, although patents clearly are property for purposes of the Fourteenth Amendment, the PRCA is not justified under Boerne v. Flores[7], which set forth standards for legislation designed to redress Fourteenth Amendment violations. In Florida Prepaid Postsecondary Education Expense Board v. College Savings Bank,[8] the Court essentially invalidated the PRCA because it "does not respond to a history of 'widespread and persisting deprivation of constitutional rights' of the sort Congress has faced in enacting property prophylactic § 5 legislation."[9] The majority was disturbed by the lack of evidence in the legislative record regarding state infringements of patents. The majority opinion also was clearly concerned with what it perceived as the broad scope of the PRCA, to the extent that Congress "made all States immediately amenable to suit in federal court for all kinds of possible patent infringement and for an indefinite duration."[10] Interestingly, in support of its position that the scope of the PRCA is too expansive, the Court criticized Congress for failing to limit the coverage of the PRCA to cases where a State refuses to offer any state-court remedy for patent owners whose patents it had infringed.[11]

In light of this opinion, it is worth pondering whether the CRCA would meet a similar fate. The dissenting opinion in *Florida Prepaid* notes that perhaps the CRCA might not be similarly invalidated because the legislative history of that statute includes many examples of copyright infringe-

[4] 517 U.S. at 46, 116 S.Ct. at 1119.

[5] 48 U.S.P.Q.2d 1481, 1487 (5th Cir. 1998).

[6] 992 F.Supp. 876, 45 U.S.P.Q.2d 1953 (N.D. Tex. 1998).

[7] 521 U.S. 507, 117 S.Ct. 2157, 138 L.Ed.2d 624 (1997).

[8] ___ U.S. ___, 119 S.Ct. 2199, ___ L.Ed.2d ___, 1999 WL 412723 (1999).

[9] Id. At p. 10 (quoting Boerne, 521 U.S. at 526).

[10] Id. At 10.

[11] Id.

ments by the States.[12] Therefore, arguably Congress was responding to widespread violations in enacting the CRCA, and this fact might be sufficient to sustain the CRCA under *Boerne*. On the other hand, would not the majority's concerns regarding the breadth of the PRCA also apply to the CRCA? Moreover, in light of the fact that federal courts have original and exclusive jurisdiction over cases involving both federal copyright and patent laws,[13] how persuasive is the Court's reasoning that the PRCA is too broad because it is not limited to instances in which a plaintiff has been unable to obtain a remedy in state court? Should Congress have been able to reasonably foresee that it would be required to consider the extent to which remedies exist in the various states for patent and copyright infringement?[14]

Add as a second paragraph to Note 4 on page 517:

Following the Supreme Court's decision in *Feltner* (see the above addition to Note 1 in this Supplement), the Ninth Circuit held that the defendant's prevailing on the narrow issue of whether the Seventh Amendment entitled him to a jury determination on statutory damages deriving from his liability for copyright infringement does not qualify him as a prevailing party for purposes of an award of attorney's fees pursuant to § 505.[15] With respect to the question of when an award of attorney's fees is appropriate under *Fogerty*, the First Circuit in Lotus Development Corp. v. Borland International Inc.[16], affirmed the district court's refusal to award the prevailing defendant attorney's fees in a case of first impression. In so holding, the appellate court stated that the lower court did not commit legal error by reasoning that "when a plaintiff prosecutes an action, in good faith, in an unsettled area of law, and with a reasonable likelihood of success, against a party with similar financial resources, the prevailing party's case for attorney's fees is weaker, whether it be a plaintiff or a defendant." [17]

---

[12] Id. At 18, n. 9 (dissenting opinion).

[13] 28 U.S.C. § 1338 (a). In contrast, federal courts do not have exclusive jurisdiction over trademark and related matters.

[14] See the dissenting opinion in *Florida Prepaid Postsecondary Education*.

[15] Columbia Pictures Television v. Krypton Broadcasting of Birmingham Inc., 152 F.3d 1171, 47 U.S.P.Q.2d 1863 (9th Cir. 1998).

[16] 140 F.3d 70, 46 U.S.P.Q.2d 1774 (1st Cir. 1998).

[17] Id. at 1777.

ASSIGNMENT 14

PREEMPTION OF STATE LAWS: THE RIGHT OF PUBLICITY AND MISAPPROPRIATION

The following case can be added to the materials in the text either in lieu of *Baltimore Orioles, Inc.* on p. 523, or following that case on p. 531 (depending upon the relevant time constraints).

The National Basketball Association and NBA Properties, Inc. v. Motorola, Inc.

United States Court of Appeals, Second Circuit, 1997.
105 F.3d 841.

■ WINTER, CIRCUIT JUDGE:

Motorola, Inc. and Sports Team Analysis and Tracking Systems ("STATS") appeal from a permanent injunction. The injunction concerns a handheld pager sold by Motorola and marketed under the name "Sports-Trax," which displays updated information of professional basketball games in progress. The injunction prohibits appellants, absent authorization from the National Basketball Association and NBA Properties, Inc. (collectively the "NBA"), from transmitting scores or other data about NBA games in progress via the pagers, STATS's site on America On–Line's computer dial-up service, or "any equivalent means."

The crux of the dispute concerns the extent to which a state law "hot-news" misappropriation claim based on International News Service v. Associated Press, 248 U.S. 215 (1918) ("INS"), survives preemption by the federal Copyright Act and whether the NBA's claim fits within the surviving INS-type claims. We hold that a narrow "hot-news" exception does survive preemption. However, we also hold that appellants' transmission of "real-time" NBA game scores and information tabulated from television and radio broadcasts of games in progress does not constitute a misappropriation of "hot news" that is the property of the NBA.

I. BACKGROUND

The facts are largely undisputed. Motorola manufactures and markets the SportsTrax paging device while STATS supplies the game information that is transmitted to the pagers. The product became available to the public in January 1996, at a retail price of about $200. SportsTrax's pager has an inch-and-a-half by inch-and-a-half screen and operates in four basic modes: "current," "statistics," "final scores" and "demonstration." It is the "current" mode that gives rise to the present dispute. In that mode, SportsTrax displays the following information on NBA games in progress: (i) the teams playing; (ii) score changes; (iii) the team in possession of the ball; (iv) whether the team is in the free-throw bonus; (v) the quarter of the game; and (vi) time remaining in the quarter. The information is updated every two to three minutes, with more frequent updates near the end of the first half and the end of the game. There is a lag of approximately two or three minutes between events in the game itself and when the information appears on the pager screen.

SportsTrax's operation relies on a "data feed" supplied by STATS reporters who watch the games on television or listen to them on the radio. The reporters key into a personal computer changes in the score and other information such as successful and missed shots, fouls, and clock updates. The information is relayed by modem to STATS's host computer, which compiles, analyzes, and formats the data for retransmission. The information is then sent to a common carrier, which then sends it via satellite to various local FM radio networks that in turn emit the signal received by the individual SportsTrax pagers.

Finding Motorola and STATS liable for misappropriation, Judge Preska entered the permanent injunction, reserved the calculation of damages for subsequent proceedings, and stayed execution of the injunction pending appeal. Motorola and STATS appeal from the injunction.

II.   THE STATE LAW MISAPPROPRIATION CLAIM

A.   Summary of Ruling

Because our disposition of the state law misappropriation claim rests in large part on preemption by the Copyright Act, our discussion necessarily goes beyond the elements of a misappropriation claim under New York law, and a summary of our ruling here will perhaps render that discussion—or at least the need for it—more understandable.

The issues before us are ones that have arisen in various forms over the course of this century as technology has steadily increased the speed and quantity of information transmission. Today, individuals at home, at work, or elsewhere, can use a computer, pager, or other device to obtain highly selective kinds of information virtually at will. *INS* was one of the first cases to address the issues raised by these technological advances, although the technology involved in that case was primitive by contemporary standards. INS involved two wire services, the Associated Press ("AP") and International News Service ("INS"), that transmitted news stories by wire to member newspapers. Id. INS would lift factual stories from AP bulletins and send them by wire to INS papers. Id. at 231. INS would also take factual stories from east coast AP papers and wire them to INS papers on the west coast that had yet to publish because of time differentials. Id. at 238. The Supreme Court held that INS's conduct was a common-law misappropriation of AP's property. Id. at 242.

With the advance of technology, radio stations began "live" broadcasts of events such as baseball games and operas, and various entrepreneurs began to use the transmissions of others in one way or another for their own profit. In response, New York courts created a body of misappropriation law, loosely based on INS, that sought to apply ethical standards to the use by one party of another's transmissions of events.

Federal copyright law played little active role in this area until 1976. Before then, it appears to have been the general understanding—there being no caselaw of consequence—that live events such as baseball games were not copyrightable. Moreover, doubt existed even as to whether a recorded broadcast or videotape of such an event was copyrightable. In 1976, however, Congress passed legislation expressly affording copyright protection to simultaneously-recorded broadcasts of live performances such as sports events. See 17 U.S.C. § 101. Such protection was not extended to the underlying events.

The 1976 amendments also contained provisions preempting state law claims that enforced rights "equivalent" to exclusive copyright protections when the work to which the state claim was being applied fell within the area of copyright protection. See 17 U.S.C. § 301. Based on legislative history of the 1976 Amendments, it is generally agreed that a "hot-news" INS-like claim survives preemption. H.R. No. 94–1476 at 132 (1976), reprinted in 1976 U.S.C.C.A.N. 5659, 5748. However, much of New York misappropriation law after INS goes well beyond "hot-news" claims and is preempted.

B.   Copyrights in Events or Broadcasts of Events

The NBA asserted copyright infringement claims with regard both to the underlying games and to their broadcasts. The district court dismissed these claims, and the NBA does not appeal from their dismissal. Nevertheless, discussion of the infringement claims is necessary to provide the framework for analyzing the viability of the NBA's state law misappropriation claim in light of the Copyright Act's preemptive effect.

1.   Infringement of a Copyright in the Underlying Games

In our view, the underlying basketball games do not fall within the subject matter of federal copyright protection because they do not constitute "original works of authorship" under 17 U.S.C. § 102(a). Sports events are not "authored" in any common sense of the word. There is, of course, at least at the professional level, considerable preparation for a game. However, the preparation is as much an expression of hope or faith as a determination of what will actually happen. Unlike movies, plays, television programs, or operas, athletic events are competitive and have no underlying script. Preparation may even cause mistakes to succeed, like the broken play in football that gains yardage because the opposition could not expect it. Athletic events may also result in wholly unanticipated occurrences, the most notable recent event being in a championship baseball game in which interference with a fly ball caused an umpire to signal erroneously a home run.

What "authorship" there is in a sports event, moreover, must be open to copying by competitors if fans are to be attracted. If the inventor of the T-formation in football had been able to copyright it, the sport might have come to an end instead of prospering. Even where athletic preparation most resembles authorship—figure skating, gymnastics, and, some would uncharitably say, professional wrestling—a performer who conceives and executes a particularly graceful and difficult—or, in the case of wrestling, seemingly painful—acrobatic feat cannot copyright it without impairing the underlying competition in the future. A claim of being the only athlete to perform a feat doesn't mean much if no one else is allowed to try.

For many of these reasons, Nimmer on Copyright concludes that the "far more reasonable" position is that athletic events are not copyrightable. 1 M. Nimmer & D. Nimmer, Nimmer on Copyright § 2.09[F] at 2–170.1 (1996). Nimmer notes that, among other problems, the number of joint copyright owners would arguably include the league, the teams, the athletes, umpires, stadium workers and even fans, who all contribute to the "work."

Concededly, caselaw is scarce on the issue of whether organized events themselves are copyrightable, but what there is indicates that they are not. See Prod. Contractors, Inc. v. WGN Continental Broad. Co., 622 F.Supp. 1500 (N.D.Ill.1985) (Christmas parade is not a work of authorship entitled to copyright protection). In claiming a copyright in the underlying games, the NBA relied in part on a footnote in Baltimore Orioles, Inc. v. Major League Baseball Players Assn., 805 F.2d 663, 669 n. 7 (7th Cir.1986), cert. denied, 480 U.S.941 (1987), which stated that the "players' performances" contain the "Modest Creativity Required for Copyrightability." However, the Court went on to state, "moreover, even if the players' performances were not sufficiently creative, the players agree that the cameramen and director contribute creative labor to the telecasts." Id. This last sentence indicates that the court was considering the copyrightability of telecasts—not the underlying games, which obviously can be played without cameras.

We believe that the lack of caselaw is attributable to a general understanding that athletic events were, and are, uncopyrightable. Indeed, prior to 1976, there was even doubt that broadcasts describing or depicting such events, which have a far stronger case for copyrightability than the events themselves, were entitled to copyright protection. Indeed, as described in the next subsection of this opinion, Congress found it necessary to extend such protection to recorded broadcasts of live events. The fact that Congress did not extend such protection to the events themselves confirms our view that the district court correctly held that appellants were not infringing a copyright in the NBA games.

2. Infringement of a Copyright in the Broadcasts of NBA Games

As noted, recorded broadcasts of NBA games—as opposed to the games themselves—are now entitled to copyright protection. The Copyright Act was amended in 1976 specifically to insure that simultaneously-recorded transmissions of live performances and sporting events would meet the Act's requirement that the original work of authorship be "fixed in any tangible medium of expression." 17 U.S.C. § 102(a). Accordingly, Section 101 of the Act, containing definitions, was amended to read:

> A work consisting of sounds, images, or both, that are being transmitted, is "fixed" for purposes of this title if a fixation of the work is being made simultaneously with its transmission.

17 U.S.C. § 101. Congress specifically had sporting events in mind:

> [T]he bill seeks to resolve, through the definition of "fixation" in section 101, the status of live broadcasts—sports, news coverage, live performances of music, etc.—that are reaching the public in unfixed form but that are simultaneously being recorded.

H.R. No. 94–1476 at 52, reprinted in 1976 U.S.C.C.A.N. at 5665. The House Report also makes clear that it is the broadcast, not the underlying game, that is the subject of copyright protection. In explaining how game broadcasts meet the Act's requirement that the subject matter be an "original work[] of authorship," 17 U.S.C. § 102(a), the House Report stated:

> When a football game is being covered by four television cameras, with a director guiding the activities of the four cameramen and choosing which of their electronic images are sent out to the public and in what order, there is little doubt that what the cameramen and the director are doing constitutes "authorship."

H.R. No. 94–1476 at 52, reprinted in 1976 U.S.C.C.A.N. at 5665.

Although the broadcasts are protected under copyright law, the district court correctly held that Motorola and STATS did not infringe NBA's copyright because they reproduced only facts from the broadcasts, not the expression or description of the game that constitutes the broadcast. The "fact/expression dichotomy" is a bedrock principle of copyright law that "limits severely the scope of protection in fact-based works." Feist Publications, Inc. v. Rural Tel. Service Co., 499 U.S. 340 (1991). " 'No author may copyright facts or ideas. The copyright is limited to those aspects of the work—termed "expression"—that display the stamp of the author's originality.' " Id. (quoting Harper & Row, Inc. v. Nation Enter., 471 U.S. 539, 547–48 (1985)).

We agree with the district court that the "defendants provide purely factual information which any patron of an NBA game could acquire from the arena without any involvement from the director, cameramen, or others who contribute to the originality of a broadcast." 939 F. Supp. at 1094. Because the SportsTrax device and AOL site reproduce only factual information culled from the broadcasts and none of the copyrightable expression of the games, appellants did not infringe the copyright of the broadcasts.

C. The State–Law Misappropriation Claim

The district court's injunction was based on its conclusion that, under New York law, defendants had unlawfully misappropriated the NBA's property rights in its games. The district court reached this conclusion by holding: (i) that the NBA's misappropriation claim relating to the underlying games was not preempted by Section 301 of the Copyright Act; and (ii) that, under New York common law, defendants had engaged in unlawful misappropriation. Id. at 1094–1107. We disagree.

1. Preemption Under the Copyright Act
a) Summary $(i) + (ii) = $ preemption of state law claim

When Congress amended the Copyright Act in 1976, it provided for the preemption of state law claims that are interrelated with copyright claims in certain ways. Under 17 U.S.C. § 301, a state law claim is preempted when: (i) the state law claim seeks to vindicate "legal or equitable rights that are equivalent" to one of the bundle of exclusive rights already protected by copyright law under 17 U.S.C. § 106—styled the "general scope requirement"; and (ii) the particular work to which the state law claim is being applied falls within the type of works protected by the Copyright Act under Sections 102 and 103—styled the "subject matter requirement."

The district court concluded that the NBA's misappropriation claim was not preempted because, with respect to the underlying games, as opposed to the broadcasts, the subject matter requirement was not met. 939 F.Supp. at 1097. The court dubbed as "partial preemption" its separate analysis of misappropriation claims relating to the underlying games and misappropriation claims relating to broadcasts of those games. Id. at 1098, n.24. The district court then relied on a series of older New York misappropriation cases involving radio broadcasts that considerably broadened INS. We hold that where the challenged copying or misappropriation relates in part to the copyrighted broadcasts of the games, the subject matter requirement is met as to both the broadcasts and the games. We therefore reject the partial preemption doctrine and its anomalous consequence that "it is possible for a plaintiff to assert claims both for infringement of its copyright in a broadcast and misappropriation of its rights in the underlying event." Id. We do find that a properly-narrowed INS "hot-news" misappropriation claim survives preemption because it fails the general scope requirement, but that the broader theory of the radio broadcast cases relied

IMPO.

upon by the district court were preempted when Congress extended copy-right protection to simultaneously-recorded broadcasts.

b) "Partial Preemption" and the Subject Matter Requirement

The subject matter requirement is met when the work of authorship being copied or misappropriated "falls within the ambit of copyright protection." Harper & Row, Inc. v. Nation Enter., 723 F.2d 195, 200 (1983), rev'd on other grounds, 471 U.S. 539 (1985). We believe that the subject matter requirement is met in the instant matter and that the concept of "partial preemption" is not consistent with section 301 of the Copyright Act. Although game broadcasts are copyrightable while the underlying games are not, the Copyright Act should not be read to distinguish between the two when analyzing the preemption of a misappropriation claim based on copying or taking from the copyrightable work. We believe that:

> [O]nce a performance is reduced to tangible form, there is no distinction between the performance and the recording of the performance for the purposes of preemption under § 301(a). Thus, if a baseball game were not broadcast [*23] or were telecast without being recorded, the Players' performances similarly would not be fixed in tangible form and their rights of publicity would not be subject to preemption. By virtue of being videotaped, however, the Players' performances are fixed in tangible form, and any rights of publicity in their performances that are equivalent to the rights contained in the copyright of the telecast are preempted.

Baltimore Orioles, 805 F.2d at 675 (citation omitted).

Copyrightable material often contains uncopyrightable elements within it, but Section 301 preemption bars state law misappropriation claims with respect to uncopyrightable as well as copyrightable elements. In Harper & Row, for example, we held that state law claims based on the copying of excerpts from President Ford's memoirs were preempted even with respect to information that was purely factual and not copyrightable. We stated:

> The [Copyright] Act clearly embraces "works of authorship," including "literary works," as within its subject matter. The fact that portions of the Ford memoirs may consist of uncopyrightable material ... does not take the work as a whole outside the subject matter [*24] protected by the Act. Were this not so, states would be free to expand the perimeters of copyright protection to their own liking, on the theory that preemption would be no bar to state protection of material not meeting federal statutory standards.

723 F.2d at 200 (citation omitted). The legislative history supports this understanding of Section 301(a)'s subject matter requirement. The House Report stated:

> As long as a work fits within one of the general subject matter categories of sections 102 and 103, the bill prevents the States from protecting it even if it fails to achieve Federal statutory copyright because it is too minimal or lacking in originality to qualify, or because it has fallen into the public domain.

H.R. No. 94–1476 at 131, reprinted in 1976 U.S.C.C.A.N. at 5747. See also Baltimore Orioles, 805 F.2d at 676 (citing excerpts of House Report 94–1476).

Adoption of a partial preemption doctrine—preemption of claims based on misappropriation of broadcasts but no preemption of claims based on misappropriation of underlying facts—would expand significantly the reach of state law claims and render the preemption intended by Congress unworkable. It is often difficult or impossible to separate the fixed copyrightable work from the underlying uncopyrightable events or facts. Moreover, Congress, in extending copyright protection only to the broadcasts and not to the underlying events, intended that the latter be in the public domain. Partial preemption turns that intent on its head by allowing state law to vest exclusive rights in material that Congress intended to be in the public domain and to make unlawful conduct that Congress intended to allow.

c) The General Scope Requirement

Under the general scope requirement, Section 301 "preempts only those state law rights that 'may be abridged by an act which, in and of itself, would infringe one of the exclusive rights' provided by federal copyright law." Computer Assoc. Int'l, Inc. v. Altai, Inc., 982 F.2d 693, 716 (2d Cir.1992) (quoting Harper & Row, 723 F.2d at 200). However, certain forms of commercial misappropriation otherwise within the general scope requirement will survive preemption if an "extra-element" test is met.

We turn, therefore, to the question of the extent to which a "hot-news" misappropriation claim based on INS involves extra elements and is not the equivalent of exclusive rights under a copyright. Courts are generally agreed that some form of such a claim survives preemption. This conclusion is based in part on the legislative history of the 1976 amendments. The House Report stated:

> "Misappropriation" is not necessarily synonymous with copyright infringement, and thus a cause of action labeled as "misappropriation" is not preempted if it is in fact based neither on a right within the general scope of copyright as specified by section 106 nor on a right equivalent thereto. For example, state law should have the flexibility to afford a remedy (under traditional principles of equity) against a consistent pattern of unauthorized appropriation by a competitor of the facts (i.e., not the literary expression) constituting "hot" news, whether in the traditional mold of International News Service v.Associated Press, 248 U.S. 215 (1918), or in the newer form of data updates from scientific, business, or financial data bases.

H.R. No. 94–1476 at 132, reprinted in 1976 U.S.C.C.A.N. at 5748 (footnote omitted). The crucial question, therefore, is the breadth of the "hot-news" claim that survives preemption.

In INS, the plaintiff AP and defendant INS were "wire services" that sold news items to client newspapers. AP brought suit to prevent INS from selling facts and information lifted from AP sources to INS-affiliated newspapers. One method by which INS was able to use AP's news was to lift facts from AP news bulletins. INS, 248 U.S. at 231. Another method was to sell facts taken from just-published east coast AP newspapers to west coast INS newspapers whose editions had yet to appear. Id. at 238. The Supreme Court held (prior to Erie R. Co. v. Tompkins, 304 U.S. 64 (1938)), that INS's use of AP's information was unlawful under federal common law. It characterized INS's conduct as

> amount[ing] to an unauthorized interference with the normal operation of complainant's legitimate business precisely at the point where the profit is to be reaped, in order to divert a material portion of the profit from those who have earned it to those who have not; with special advantage to defendant in the competition because of the fact that it is not burdened with any part of the expense of gathering the news.

INS, 248 U.S. at 240.

The theory of the New York misappropriation cases relied upon by the district court is considerably broader than that of INS. For example, the district court quoted at length from Metropolitan Opera Ass'n v. Wagner–Nichols Recorder Corp., 199 Misc. 786, 101 N.Y.S.2d 483 (N.Y.Sup.Ct. 1950), aff'd, 279 A.D. 632, 107 N.Y.S.2d 795 (1st Dep't 1951). Metropolitan Opera described New York misappropriation law as standing for the "broader principle that property rights of commercial value are to be and will be protected from any form of commercial immorality"; that misappropriation law developed "to deal with business malpractices offensive to the ethics of [ ] society"; and that the doctrine is "broad and flexible." 939 F. Supp. at 1098–1110 (quoting Metropolitan Opera, 101 N.Y.S.2d at 492, 488–89).

However, we believe that Metropolitan Opera's broad misappropriation doctrine based on amorphous concepts such as "commercial immorality" or society's "ethics" is preempted. Such concepts are virtually synonymous for wrongful copying and are in no meaningful fashion distinguishable from infringement of a copyright. The broad misappropriation doctrine relied upon by the district court is, therefore, the equivalent of exclusive rights in copyright law.

Most of the broadcast cases relied upon by the NBA are simply not good law. Those cases were decided at a time when simultaneously-recorded broadcasts were not protected under the Copyright Act and when the state law claims they fashioned were not subject to federal preemption. For example, Metropolitan Opera, 199 Misc. 786, 101 N.Y.S.2d 483, involved the unauthorized copying, marketing, and sale of opera radio broadcasts. As another example, in Mutual Broadcasting System v. Muzak Corp.,177 Misc. 489, 30 N.Y.S.2d 419 (Sup. Ct. 1941), the defendant simultaneously retransmitted the plaintiff's baseball radio broadcasts onto telephone lines.

As discussed above, the 1976 amendments to the Copyright Act were specifically designed to afford copyright protection to simultaneously-recorded broadcasts, and Metropolitan Opera and Muzak could today be brought as copyright infringement cases. Moreover, we believe that they would have to be brought as copyright cases because the amendments affording broadcasts copyright protection also preempted the state law misappropriation claims under which they were decided.

Our conclusion, therefore, is that only a narrow "hot-news" misappropriation claim survives preemption for actions concerning material within the realm of copyright. In our view, the elements central to an INS claim are: (i) the plaintiff generates or collects information at some cost or expense, (ii) the value of the information is highly time-sensitive, (iii) the defendant's use of the information constitutes free-riding on the plaintiff's costly efforts to generate or collect it; (iv) the defendant's use of the information is in direct competition with a product or service offered by the plaintiff, [and] (v) the ability of other parties to free-ride on the efforts of the plaintiff would so reduce the incentive to produce the product or service that its existence or quality would be substantially threatened.

INS is not about ethics; it is about the protection of property rights in time-sensitive information so that the information will be made available to the public by profit-seeking entrepreneurs. If services like AP were not assured of property rights in the news they pay to collect, they would cease to collect it. The ability of their competitors to appropriate their product at only nominal cost and thereby to disseminate a competing product at a lower price would destroy the incentive to collect news in the first place. The newspaper-reading public would suffer because no one would have an incentive to collect "hot news."

We therefore find the extra elements—those in addition to the elements of copyright infringement—that allow a "hotnews" claim to survive preemption are: (i) the time-sensitive value of factual information, (ii) the free-riding by a defendant, and (iii) the threat to the very existence of the product or service provided by the plaintiff.

2.   The Legality of SportsTrax

We conclude that Motorola and STATS have not engaged in unlawful misappropriation under the "hot-news" test set out above. To be sure, some of the elements of a "hot-news" INS-claim are met. The information transmitted to SportsTrax is not precisely contemporaneous, but it is nevertheless time-sensitive. Also, the NBA does provide, or will shortly do so, information like that available through SportsTrax. It now offers a service called "Gamestats" that provides official play-by-play game sheets and half-time and final box scores within each arena. It also provides such information to the media in each arena. In the future, the NBA plans to enhance Gamestats so that it will be networked between the various arenas and will support a pager product analogous to SportsTrax. SportsTrax will of course directly compete with an enhanced Gamestats.

However, there are critical elements missing in the NBA's attempt to assert a "hot-news" INS-type claim. As framed by the NBA, their claim compresses and confuses three different informational products. The first product is generating the information by playing the games; the second product is transmitting live, full descriptions of those games; and the third product is collecting and retransmitting strictly factual information about the games. The first and second products are the NBA's primary business: producing basketball games for live attendance and licensing copyrighted broadcasts of those games. The collection and retransmission of strictly factual material about the games is a different product: e.g., box-scores in newspapers, summaries of statistics on television sports news, and real-time facts to be transmitted to pagers. In our view, the NBA has failed to show any competitive effect whatsoever from SportsTrax on the first and second products and a lack of any free-riding by SportsTrax on the third.

With regard to the NBA's primary products—producing basketball games with live attendance and licensing copyrighted broadcasts of those games—there is no evidence that anyone regards SportsTrax as a substitute for attending NBA games or watching them on television. In fact, Motorola markets SportsTrax as being designed "for those times when you cannot be at the arena, watch the game on TV, or listen to the radio ..."

The NBA argues that the pager market is also relevant to a "hot-news" INS-type claim and that SportsTrax's future competition with Gamestats satisfies any missing element. We agree that there is a separate market for the real-time transmission of factual information to pagers or similar devices. However, we disagree that SportsTrax is in any sense free-riding off Gamestats.

An indispensable element of an INS "hot-news" claim is free-riding by a defendant on a plaintiff's product, enabling the defendant to produce a directly competitive product for less money because it has lower costs. SportsTrax is not such a product. The use of pagers to transmit real-time information about NBA games requires: (i) the collecting of facts about the games; (ii) the transmission of these facts on a network; (iii) the assembling of them by the particular service; and (iv) the transmission of them to pagers or an on-line computer site. Appellants are in no way free-riding on Gamestats. Motorola and STATS expend their own resources to collect purely factual information generated in NBA games to transmit to Sports-Trax pagers. They have their own network and assemble and transmit data themselves.

SportsTrax and Gamestats are each bearing their own costs of collecting factual information on NBA games, and, if one produces a product that is cheaper or otherwise superior to the other, that producer will prevail in the marketplace. This is obviously not the situation against which INS was intended to prevent: the potential lack of any such product or service because of the anticipation of free-riding.

For the foregoing reasons, the NBA has not shown any damage to any of its products based on free-riding by Motorola and STATS, and the NBA's misappropriation claim based on New York law is preempted.

IV. CONCLUSION

We vacate the injunction entered by the district court and order that the NBA's claim for misappropriation be dismissed.

Add the following paragraph based on *N.B.A. v. Motorola* at the end of Note 1 on p. 544:

Baltimore Orioles and *N.B.A. v. Motorola* both reject a partial preemption analysis when dealing with state law claims involving both non-copyrightable subject matter such as athletic events and copyrightable subject matter such as the broadcasts of these events. These courts determined that the misappropriation claims based on the uncopyrightable matter still could be preempted in situations where the non-copyrightable matter is fixed and the misappropriation claim is based on copying from the copyrightable work. Do you agree with this analysis? In *N.B.A. v. Motorola*, the court bolstered its conclusion by saying that "partial preemption" allows "state law to vest exclusive rights in material that Congress intended to be in the public domain and to make unlawful conduct that Congress intended to allow." Given that what was at issue in *Motorola* was the appropriation of factual material, in what way is the analysis in *Baltimore Orioles* less defensible?

Add the following at the end of Note 3 on p. 546:

In *N.B.A. v. Motorola,* the court provided clear guidance on when a misappropriation involving "hot-news" would escape preemption. Did you agree with the court's application of its exception to the facts at issue? Recall the *Dow Jones* cases reprinted in Assignment 3B. Is that case still good law after *Motorola*?

Add the following paragraphs at the end of Note 6 on page 549:

In Allison v. Vintage Sports Plaques,[1] the Eleventh Circuit held, in a case of first impression, that the first sale doctrine applies to limit the common law right of publicity under Alabama law. The court reasoned that such an application of the first sale doctrine would not impact significantly upon a celebrity's right to license the use of her image because she still has the right to make this determination initially and thus enjoy the ability to determine when, or if, her image will be distributed.[2] Thus, the court concluded that the first sale doctrine barred publicity claims based on the

---

[1] 136 F.3d 1443, 46 U.S.P.Q.2d 1138 (11th Cir. 1998). [2] Id. at 1143.

defendants' production and sale of plaques featuring mounted sports trading cards displaying plaintiffs' names and likenesses.

Wendt v. Host International, Inc.[3] raised many interesting right of publicity issues before the Ninth Circuit. In that case, actors George Wendt and John Ratzenberger sued Host for violating their rights of publicity by creating animatronic robotic figures based upon their likenesses and placing these robots in airport bars that were modeled upon the set from the television program *Cheers*. The district court dismissed the action but the Ninth Circuit held that the likeness determination is an issue for resolution by the jury. In so holding, the court rejected the defendants' argument that since the robots only appropriate the identities of the characters played by the actors, the plaintiffs cannot claim a right of publicity violation by relying on indicia such as the set of the *Cheers* Bar that are the property of Paramount, the producer of *Cheers* and owner of the copyright to the television program. The plaintiffs argued that although they do not have any rights to the characters themselves, the physical likeness of the robots to the actors is what has commercial value to Host.

As *Wendt* illustrates, several difficulties arise when right of publicity claims implicate the appropriation of characters portrayed by actors. Should the rights at issue be considered the property of the persona (Wendt and Ratzenberger) or the entity producing the work in which the persona appears (Paramount)? Does it depend upon how many other roles the persona in question has played? If protection is afforded to the persona in these instances, is there a risk that the law is overly protecting the persona's interest to the detriment of those who make considerable creative contributions to the work in which the persona appears? Should the persona's contribution be treated analogously to a work made for hire under copyright law? Should these claims be preempted under the 1976 Copyright Act?

Insert the following as Note 8 on page 550:

8. *The Right of Publicity and the Digital Dilemma.* Digital technology is creating endless possibilities for right of publicity litigation. For example, in Hoffman v. Capital Cities/ABC Inc.,[4] the defendant magazine was found liable under both the common law as well as the California right of publicity statute for publishing a photograph of actor Dustin Hoffman as he appeared in the 1982 movie *Tootsie*. The photograph, however, was digitally altered so that Mr. Hoffman appeared to be wearing a gown designed by Richard Tyler and shoes designed by Ralph Lauren, accompanied by the following text: "Dustin Hoffman isn't a drag in butter-colored silk gown by Richard Tyler and Ralph Lauren heels."[5]

---

[3] 125 F.3d 806 (9th Cir. 1997).

[4] 33 F.Supp.2d 867, 50 U.S.P.Q.2d 1195 (C.D.Cal. 1999).

[5] Id. at 1198.

Currently, a debate is being waged in the California legislature regarding the Burton Bill, which would dramatically expand the scope of publicity rights for deceased celebrities by eliminating the current list of exemptions in California's right of publicity statute for plays, books, and other genres typically protected by the First Amendment. The proposed bill would replace these exemptions with a presumption of control in the heirs of deceased celebrities subject to the First Amendment's strictures of free speech. Actor Richard Masur, the President of the Screen Actors Guild, testified before the California Senate that new digital technology adds greater urgency to the need for stronger publicity rights. Representative of this technology is a process called "morphing", computer manipulation of old images in which deceased individuals are transformed into live characters in films and videos (the movie *Forest Gump* invoked this technology). Opponents of this bill worry that its enactment will stifle creativity and cause much uncertainty regarding the scope of appropriate protection for celebrity.[6]

The unauthorized use of celebrity names and likenesses on the Internet also is becoming an increasingly unmanageable problem. Consider the plight of Pamela Anderson Lee, whose name allegedly appears on more than 145,000 web pages, most of which are marketing products or services with no legitimate relationship to the actress. Internet technology makes it possible to embed hidden words—called "meta tags"–in the computer programming that underlies a webcite. These meta tags affect the way a cite is indexed by search engines. Many web page creators elect to list "Pamela Anderson Lee" among the meta tags regarding their site's actual topic, given the reality that her name will be a tremendous drawing card. Of course, the parallel between this practice and that of using celebrity names and likenesses without authorization on the cover of magazines or on T-shirts is obvious. The interesting twist regarding such usage in cyberspace, however, is that it can be accomplished with tremendous ease and on a large-scale.[7]

9. *Private alternatives to copyright protection: contracts and Article 2B of the Uniform Commercial Code.* The high cost of developing materials like databases and computer programs, which are either uncopyrightable or thinly copyrighted, has led to considerable interest in developing private alternatives to the protection afforded by statutory intellectual property laws.

a. *Contracts.* One alternative—or supplement—to statutory protection is the so-called shrinkwrap (or end-use) license. This is an agreement that is encountered during the first use of a product. Typically, it is found on the wrapper of the product; with software, it will often appear on the

---

[6] Vincent J. Schodolski, *Heirs Seek Right to Screen Use of Celebrity Images,* Chi. Trib., Apr. 26,1999 at 11.

[7] Thomas E. Weber, *Net of Fame: Who Rules the Web? Pamela Anderson Lee, The B–Movie Actress,* Wall St. J., April 13, 1999, at A1.

first screen seen when the program is loaded onto a computer. Accessing the product—tearing the wrapper or clicking through the initial screen—is deemed to be consent to the terms of the agreement. When these agreements are enforceable, licensors can use them to acquire many of the advantages of copyright. They can, for example, secure payment for continued use of a work. They can also impose prohibitions on use that mirror activities that would be regarded as copyright infringement were the product copyrighted, such as limits on copying, distribution, or preparation of derivative works. Shrinkwrap license can also be used to restrict licensees in ways that are not contemplated by the Copyright Act. For instance, a license could prohibit uses that would be considered fair under § 107, or compulsory under § 110. Since the product is considered sold rather than licensed, the licensor can also bar resales that would be permitted under § 109(a).

For a long time, shrinkwrap licenses were thought unenforceable on two grounds: first, as adhesive under traditional contracts law, or second, as preempted by federal copyright law. However, in a decision that many see as the beginning of a new trend, an important circuit—the Seventh—in an opinion by an important judge—Frank Easterbrook—enforced a shrinkwrap license. The product in ProCD Inc. v. Zeidenberg[8] was a database of telephone numbers inscribed on a CD. Zeidenberg acquired the product subject to an agreement that the database could be put only to personal uses. He nonetheless resold the information in the database commercially and ProCD sued. In upholding the agreement, the court reasoned that the "licensee" had an opportunity to review the contract and reject the product if he found the terms unacceptable. Zeidenberg's continued use of the CD could, therefore, be construed as acceptance of the terms of the agreement under § 2–606(1)(b) of the Uniform Commercial Code.[9] As to preemption, the court noted that the contract affected only the parties to the agreement and not the world at large. As such, its "rights" were not equivalent to copyright, and were therefore not preempted under § 301(a).[10]

b. *Article 2B of the Uniform Commercial Code.* For several years, the American Law Institute (ALI) and the National Conference of Commissioners on Uniform State Laws (NCCUSL) have worked on a new Article to be added to the Uniform Commercial Code. Denominated "2B," this Article was to cover the licensing of intangible products.[11] The project began in an attempt to modify the UCC's requirements of writings, signatures, and the like to the on-line environment, where transactions are consummated electronically, at the click of a mouse. The initial work was later expanded to cover transactions in software, whether involving the exchange of hard copy or through electronic transmission. The theory was that Art. 2's heavy

---

[8] 86 F.3d 1447 (7th Cir. 1996).

[9] Id. at 1452.

[10] Id. at 1454.

[11] For those whose memory of contracts is hazy, Art. 2 covers the sale of goods. The ALI and NCCUSL are also considering an Art. 2A, which will cover services.

focus on such physical issues as delivery, inspection, and conformity make it inapposite to software transactions. Next, the drafters decided that this theory applied to all intangibles. Accordingly, they decided to broaden Art. 2B to all transactions in "information."

Article 2B adopted the core principles of the Uniform Commercial Code. As is the case in Art. 2 on goods, Art. 2B was biased in favor of contract-formation and its guiding principle was party autonomy. The Article was intended to reduce transaction costs by supplying off-the-shelf terms that parties can adopt for free. Moreover, it "saved" contracts that would otherwise fail for the omission of key terms. That is, under Art. 2B, a contract could be formed without an agreement as to all of its terms; if an omitted term became relevant to a dispute, the provisions of the Article would act as default rules. With a few exceptions directed at protecting consumers, the provisions could be altered by agreement of the parties.

According to its drafters, Art. 2B was not intended to create intellectual property rights, but rather to facilitate licensing. Nonetheless, it came under heavy criticism as inconsistent with national innovation policy. As in *ProCD*, Art. 2B would permit licensing even in situations where there is an inequality of bargaining power and no opportunity for meaningful negotiation. It would facilitate not only the kind of licensing contemplated by federal law, but also licenses over non-protectable subject matter and licenses that preclude activities permissible under the Copyright Act. Opponents of the Article were, therefore, worried that the Article would lead to an increase in the number of transactions that prevent usages that the public would otherwise enjoy at no (or reduced) cost. For example, it is difficult to see why anyone would sell a book and give the purchaser a right to resell, when the same book could as easily be "licensed" in a way that preserves the copyright owner's plenary control over further sales.[12] Similarly, why sell a sound recording when a license could be used to create an obligation to pay for every performance?

The Article specifically stated that any provision of the Article or any provision of a contract that is inconsistent with federal law would be unenforceable. However, the statement was considered ineffective. The Article would largely be enforced by state courts. Although these courts are somewhat unfamiliar with intellectual property policy (remember, copyright, patent, and trademark infringement is in the exclusive jurisdiction of federal courts[13]), the Article provided very little guidance on preemption principles. In fact, the drafters repeatedly cited *ProCD*'s notion that rights against individual parties are different from rights against the world; nowhere did they grapple with the fact that the facilitation of bilateral agreements can create cumulative effects that duplicate the impact of rights against the world.

---

[12] See, e.g., David A. Rice, Digital Information as Property and Product: U.C.C. Article 2B, 22 Dayton L. Rev. 621 (1997).

[13] 28 U.S.C. § 1338.

In addition to these general observations on the effect of the Article on innovation policy, specific industries began to express concern that the default rules do not reflect their traditional practices, and that the Article could raise transaction costs by requiring the parties to a license to specifically contract out of each provision of the Article that is inconsistent with expectations based on prior experience. In response to these concerns, the drafters began to carve exceptions into the scope provision—to except, for example, a license of a trademark, a nonsoftware patent or related know-how, a contract for entertainment services (except for software development), a license of a linear motion picture or sound recording, or a license of a regularly scheduled audio or video programming by a broadcast, cable, or similar programming service.

Needless to say, this complicated scope provision raised concerns of its own. Consider, for example, a contract to license a video game: part of the contract will deal with trademarks, part with software (patents and copyrights), part with other patents; some of the agreement may deal with know how, some of which may be related to the software patents, some related to nonsoftware patents, and some may be classified as free-standing trade secrets. With a complicated scope provision like the one contemplated, it would be difficult for the parties to this contract to predict which parts of the agreement are controlled by Art. 2B, which parts by other provisions of the UCC, and which by common law or another state statute. Furthermore, because the statute had no safe harbor provisions, parties would also need to worry about whether matters that they specifically bargained for would be enforceable after a preemption challenge.

These concerns have recently led to major changes in direction. After NCCUSL decided against various amendments suggested by members of the ALI (largely related to public interest safeguards), the ALI pulled out of the project. But since the UCC has always been a joint effort of both of these organizations, Art. 2B could no longer be situated within the Uniform Commercial Code. Renamed "UCITA"—the Uniform Computer Information Transactions Act—the Article will be propounded as a stand-alone law, dealing mainly with software sales and licensing. NCCUSL plans to vote it out in July 1999, at which point the states will begin to consider its adoption.

ASSIGNMENT 16

SUBJECT MATTER

Insert on page 583, where the case can be read in lieu of *In Re Alappat* and *In Re Grams*, pages 583–597, and in conjunction with Note 1 in the text and with Notes 2 and 3 as they appear below. Alternatively, insert at page 597 and read in addition to the other computer cases.

State Street Bank & Trust Co. v. Signature Financial Group, Inc.

United States Court of Appeals for the Federal Circuit, 1998.
149 F.3d 1368.

■ RICH, CIRCUIT JUDGE.

Signature Financial Group, Inc. (Signature) [assignee of U.S. Patent No. 5,193,056 (the '056 patent), which issued to R. Todd Boes] appeals from the decision of the United States District Court for the District of Massachusetts granting a motion for summary judgment in favor of State Street Bank & Trust Co. (State Street), finding the '056 invalid on the ground that the claimed subject matter is not encompassed by 35 U.S.C. § 101 (1994). See State Street Bank & Trust Co. v. Signature Financial Group, Inc., 927 F.Supp. 502, 38 USPQ2d 1530 (D.Mass.1996). We reverse and remand because we conclude that the patent claims are directed to statutory subject matter.

DISCUSSION

The following facts pertinent to the statutory subject matter issue are either undisputed or represent the version alleged by the nonmovant. The patented invention relates generally to a system that allows an administrator to monitor and record the financial information flow and make all calculations necessary for maintaining a partner fund financial services configuration. A partner fund financial services configuration essentially allows several mutual funds, or "Spokes," to pool their investment funds into a single portfolio, or "Hub," allowing for consolidation of, inter alia, the costs of administering the fund combined with the tax advantages of a partnership. In particular, this system provides means for a daily allocation of assets for two or more Spokes that are invested in the same Hub. The system determines the percentage share that each Spoke maintains in the Hub, while taking into consideration daily changes both in the value of the

Hub's investment securities and in the concomitant amount of each Spoke's assets.

In determining daily changes, the system also allows for the allocation among the Spokes of the Hub's daily income, expenses, and net realized and unrealized gain or loss, calculating each day's total investments based on the concept of a book capital account. This enables the determination of a true asset value of each Spoke and accurate calculation of allocation ratios between or among the Spokes. The system additionally tracks all the relevant data determined on a daily basis for the Hub and each Spoke, so that aggregate year end income, expenses, and capital gain or loss can be determined for accounting and for tax purposes for the Hub and, as a result, for each publicly traded Spoke.

It is essential that these calculations are quickly and accurately performed. In large part this is required because each Spoke sells shares to the public and the price of those shares is substantially based on the Spoke's percentage interest in the portfolio. In some instances, a mutual fund administrator is required to calculate the value of the shares to the nearest penny within as little as an hour and a half after the market closes. Given the complexity of the calculations, a computer or equivalent device is a virtual necessity to perform the task.

The '056 patent application was filed 11 March 1991. It initially contained six "machine" claims, which incorporated means-plus-function clauses, and six method claims. According to Signature, during prosecution the examiner contemplated a § 101 rejection for failure to claim statutory subject matter. However, upon cancellation of the six method claims, the examiner issued a notice of allowance for the remaining present six claims on appeal. Only claim 1 is an independent claim.

The district court began its analysis by construing the claims to be directed to a process, with each "means" clause merely representing a step in that process. However, "machine" claims having "means" clauses may only be reasonably viewed as process claims if there is no supporting structure in the written description that corresponds to the claimed "means" elements. See In re Alappat, 33 F.3d 1526, 1540–41, 31 USPQ2d 1545, 1554 (Fed.Cir.1994) (in banc). This is not the case now before us.

When independent claim 1 is properly construed in accordance with § 112, ¶ 6, it is directed to a machine, as demonstrated below, where representative claim 1 is set forth, the subject matter in brackets stating the structure the written description discloses as corresponding to the respective "means" recited in the claims.

> 1. A data processing system for managing a financial services configuration of a portfolio established as a partnership, each partner being one of a plurality of funds, comprising:
>
> (a) computer processor means [a personal computer including a CPU] for processing data;

(b) storage means [a data disk] for storing data on a storage medium;

(c) first means [an arithmetic logic circuit configured to prepare the data disk to magnetically store selected data] for initializing the storage medium;

(d) second means [an arithmetic logic circuit configured to retrieve information from a specific file, calculate incremental increases or decreases based on specific input, allocate the results on a percentage basis, and store the output in a separate file] for processing data regarding assets in the portfolio and each of the funds from a previous day and data regarding increases or decreases in each of the funds, [sic, funds'] assets and for allocating the percentage share that each fund holds in the portfolio;

(e) third means [an arithmetic logic circuit configured to retrieve information from a specific file, calculate incremental increases and decreases based on specific input, allocate the results on a percentage basis and store the output in a separate file] for processing data regarding daily incremental income, expenses, and net realized gain or loss for the portfolio and for allocating such data among each fund;

(f) fourth means [an arithmetic logic circuit configured to retrieve information from a specific file, calculate incremental increases and decreases based on specific input, allocate the results on a percentage basis and store the output in a separate file] for processing data regarding daily net unrealized gain or loss for the portfolio and for allocating such data among each fund; and

(g) fifth means [an arithmetic logic circuit configured to retrieve information from specific files, calculate that information on an aggregate basis and store the output in a separate file] for processing data regarding aggregate year-end income, expenses, and capital gain or loss for the portfolio and each of the funds.

Each claim component, recited as a "means" plus its function, is to be read, of course, pursuant to § 112, ¶ 6, as inclusive of the "equivalents" of the structures disclosed in the written description portion of the specification. Thus, claim 1, properly construed, claims a machine, namely, a data processing system for managing a financial services configuration of a portfolio established as a partnership, which machine is made up of, at the very least, the specific structures disclosed in the written description and corresponding to the means-plus-function elements (a)-(g) recited in the claim. A "machine" is proper statutory subject matter under § 101. We note that, for the purposes of a § 101 analysis, it is of little relevance whether claim 1 is directed to a "machine" or a "process," as long as it falls within at least one of the four enumerated categories of patentable subject matter, "machine" and "process" being such categories.

This does not end our analysis, however, because the court concluded that the claimed subject matter fell into one of two alternative judicially-created exceptions to statutory subject matter. The court refers to the first exception as the "mathematical algorithm" exception and the second exception as the "business method" exception. Section 101 reads:

> Whoever invents or discovers any new and useful process, machine, manufacture, or composition of matter, or any new and useful improvement thereof, may obtain a patent therefor, subject to the conditions and requirements of this title.

The plain and unambiguous meaning of § 101 is that any invention falling within one of the four stated categories of statutory subject matter may be patented, provided it meets the other requirements for patentability set forth in Title 35, i.e., those found in §§ 102, 103, and 112, ¶ 2.

The repetitive use of the expansive term "any" in § 101 shows Congress's intent not to place any restrictions on the subject matter for which a patent may be obtained beyond those specifically recited in § 101. Indeed, the Supreme Court has acknowledged that Congress intended § 101 to extend to "anything under the sun that is made by man." Diamond v. Chakrabarty, 447 U.S. 303, 309, 100 S.Ct. 2204, 65 L.Ed.2d 144 (1980); see also Diamond v. Diehr, 450 U.S. 175, 182, 101 S.Ct. 1048, 67 L.Ed.2d 155 (1981). Thus, it is improper to read limitations into '101 on the subject matter that may be patented where the legislative history indicates that Congress clearly did not intend such limitations.

The "Mathematical Algorithm" Exception

The Supreme Court has identified three categories of subject matter that are unpatentable, namely "laws of nature, natural phenomena, and abstract ideas." Diehr, 450 U.S. at 185, 101 S.Ct. 1048. Of particular relevance to this case, the Court has held that mathematical algorithms are not patentable subject matter to the extent that they are merely abstract ideas. See Diehr, 450 U.S. 175, 101 S.Ct. 1048, passim; Parker v. Flook, 437 U.S. 584, 98 S.Ct. 2522, 57 L.Ed.2d 451 (1978); Gottschalk v. Benson, 409 U.S. 63, 93 S.Ct. 253, 34 L.Ed.2d 273 (1972).[1] In Diehr, the Court explained that certain types of mathematical subject matter, standing alone, represent nothing more than abstract ideas until reduced to some type of practical application, i.e., "a useful, concrete and tangible result." Alappat, 33 F.3d at 1544, 31 USPQ2d at 1557.[2]

Unpatentable mathematical algorithms are identifiable by showing they are merely abstract ideas constituting disembodied concepts or truths that are not "useful." From a practical standpoint, this means that to be patentable an algorithm must be applied in a "useful" way. In Alappat, we held that data, transformed by a machine through a series of mathematical calculations to produce a smooth waveform display on a rasterizer monitor,

---

[1] [*Gottschalk, Parker*, and *Diehr*, the Supreme Court's three attempts to deal with the question whether computer programs are patentable subject matter, are also discussed in Note 2, infra, along with the tests for patentability propounded in their aftermath by the lower courts.—eds.]

[2] This has come to be known as the mathematical algorithm exception. This designation has led to some confusion, especially given the Freeman-Walter–Abele analysis [see infra]. By keeping in mind that the mathematical algorithm is unpatentable only to the extent that it represents an abstract idea, this confusion may be ameliorated.

constituted a practical application of an abstract idea (a mathematical algorithm, formula, or calculation), because it produced "a useful, concrete and tangible result"—the smooth waveform.

Similarly, in Arrhythmia Research Technology Inc. v. Corazonix Corp., 958 F.2d 1053, 22 USPQ2d 1033 (Fed.Cir.1992), we held that the transformation of electrocardiograph signals from a patient's heartbeat by a machine through a series of mathematical calculations constituted a practical application of an abstract idea (a mathematical algorithm, formula, or calculation), because it corresponded to a useful, concrete or tangible thing—the condition of a patient's heart.

Today, we hold that the transformation of data, representing discrete dollar amounts, by a machine through a series of mathematical calculations into a final share price, constitutes a practical application of a mathematical algorithm, formula, or calculation, because it produces "a useful, concrete and tangible result"—a final share price momentarily fixed for recording and reporting purposes and even accepted and relied upon by regulatory authorities and in subsequent trades.

The district court erred by applying the Freeman–Walter–Abele test to determine whether the claimed subject matter was an unpatentable abstract idea. The Freeman–Walter–Abele test was designed by the Court of Customs and Patent Appeals, and subsequently adopted by this court, to extract and identify unpatentable mathematical algorithms in the aftermath of Benson and Flook. See In re Freeman, 573 F.2d 1237, 197 USPQ 464 (CCPA 1978) as modified by In re Walter, 618 F.2d 758, 205 USPQ 397 (CCPA 1980). The test has been thus articulated:

> First, the claim is analyzed to determine whether a mathematical algorithm is directly or indirectly recited. Next, if a mathematical algorithm is found, the claim as a whole is further analyzed to determine whether the algorithm is "applied in any manner to physical elements or process steps," and, if it is, it "passes muster under § 101."

In re Pardo, 684 F.2d 912, 915, 214 USPQ 673, 675–76 (CCPA 1982) (citing In re Abele, 684 F.2d 902, 214 USPQ 682 (CCPA 1982)).

After Diehr and Chakrabarty, the Freeman–Walter–Abele test has little, if any, applicability to determining the presence of statutory subject matter. As we pointed out in Alappat, 33 F.3d at 1543, 31 USPQ2d at 1557, application of the test could be misleading, because a process, machine, manufacture, or composition of matter employing a law of nature, natural phenomenon, or abstract idea is patentable subject matter even though a law of nature, natural phenomenon, or abstract idea would not, by itself, be entitled to such protection. The test determines the presence of, for example, an algorithm. Under Benson, this may have been a sufficient indicium of nonstatutory subject matter. However, after Diehr and Alappat, the mere fact that a claimed invention involves inputting numbers, calculating numbers, outputting numbers, and storing numbers, in and of itself, would not render it nonstatutory subject matter, unless, of course, its operation does not produce a "useful, concrete and tangible result." Alappat, 33 F.3d at 1544, 31 USPQ2d at 1557. After all, as we have repeatedly stated,

> every step-by-step process, be it electronic or chemical or mechanical, involves an algorithm in the broad sense of the term. Since § 101 expressly includes processes as a category of inventions which may be patented and § 100(b) further defines the word "process" as meaning "process, art or method, and includes a new use of a known process, machine, manufacture, composition of matter, or material," it follows that it is no ground for holding a claim is directed to nonstatutory subject matter to say it includes or is directed to an algorithm. This is why the proscription against patenting has been limited to mathematical algorithms. . . .

In re Iwahashi, 888 F.2d 1370, 1374, 12 USPQ2d 1908, 1911 (Fed.Cir. 1989).

The question of whether a claim encompasses statutory subject matter should not focus on which of the four categories of subject matter a claim is directed to—process, machine, manufacture, or composition of matterBbut rather on the essential characteristics of the subject matter, in particular, its practical utility. Section 101 specifies that statutory subject matter must also satisfy the other "conditions and requirements" of Title 35, including novelty, nonobviousness, and adequacy of disclosure and notice. See In re Warmerdam, 33 F.3d 1354, 1359, 31 USPQ2d 1754, 1757–58 (Fed.Cir. 1994). For purpose of our analysis, as noted above, claim 1 is directed to a machine programmed with the Hub and Spoke software and admittedly produces a "useful, concrete, and tangible result." Alappat, 33 F.3d at 1544, 31 USPQ2d at 1557. This renders it statutory subject matter, even if the useful result is expressed in numbers, such as price, profit, percentage, cost, or loss.

The Business Method Exception

As an alternative ground for invalidating the '056 patent under § 101, the court relied on the judicially-created, so-called "business method" exception to statutory subject matter. We take this opportunity to lay this ill-conceived exception to rest. Since its inception, the "business method" exception has merely represented the application of some general, but no longer applicable legal principle, perhaps arising out of the "requirement for invention"—which was eliminated by § 103. Since the 1952 Patent Act, business methods have been, and should have been, subject to the same legal requirements for patentability as applied to any other process or method.

The business method exception has never been invoked by this court, or the CCPA, to deem an invention unpatentable. Application of this particular exception has always been preceded by a ruling based on some clearer concept of Title 35 or, more commonly, application of the abstract idea exception based on finding a mathematical algorithm.

State Street argues that we acknowledged the validity of the business method exception in Alappat when we discussed Maucorps and Meyer:

> Maucorps dealt with a business methodology for deciding how salesmen should best handle respective customers and Meyer involved a "system" for aiding a neurologist in diagnosing patients. Clearly, neither of the alleged "inventions" in those cases falls within any § 101 category.

Alappat, 33 F.3d at 1541, 31 USPQ2d at 1555. However, closer scrutiny of these cases reveals that the claimed inventions in both Maucorps and Meyer were rejected as abstract ideas under the mathematical algorithm exception, not the business method exception. See In re Maucorps, 609 F.2d 481, 484, 203 USPQ 812, 816 (CCPA 1979); In re Meyer, 688 F.2d 789, 796, 215 USPQ 193, 199 (CCPA 1982).

Even the case frequently cited as establishing the business method exception to statutory subject matter, Hotel Security Checking Co. v. Lorraine Co., 160 F. 467 (2d Cir.1908), did not rely on the exception to strike the patent. In that case, the patent was found invalid for lack of novelty and "invention," not because it was improper subject matter for a patent. The court stated "the fundamental principle of the system is as old as the art of bookkeeping, i.e., charging the goods of the employer to the agent who takes them." Id. at 469. "If at the time of [the patent] application, there had been no system of bookkeeping of any kind in restaurants, we would be confronted with the question whether a new and useful system of cash registering and account checking is such an art as is patentable under the statute." Id. at 472.

This case is no exception. The district court announced the precepts of the business method exception as set forth in several treatises, but noted as its primary reason for finding the patent invalid under the business method exception as follows:

> If Signature's invention were patentable, any financial institution desirous of implementing a multi-tiered funding complex modelled (sic) on a Hub and Spoke configuration would be required to seek Signature's permission before embarking on such a project. This is so because the '056 Patent is claimed [sic] sufficiently broadly to foreclose virtually any computer-implemented accounting method necessary to manage this type of financial structure.

927 F.Supp. 502, 516, 38 USPQ2d 1530, 1542. Whether the patent's claims are too broad to be patentable is not to be judged under § 101, but rather under §§ 102, 103 and 112. Assuming the above statement to be correct, it has nothing to do with whether what is claimed is statutory subject matter.

In view of this background, it comes as no surprise that in the most recent edition of the Manual of Patent Examining Procedures (MPEP) (1996), a paragraph of § 706.03(a) was deleted. In past editions it read:

> Though seemingly within the category of process or method, a method of doing business can be rejected as not being within the statutory classes.

See Hotel Security Checking Co. v. Lorraine Co., 160 F. 467 (2nd Cir.1908) and In re Wait, 24 USPQ 88, 22 C.C.P.A. 822, 73 F.2d 982 (1934).

MPEP § 706.03(a) (1994). This acknowledgment is buttressed by the U.S. Patent and Trademark 1996 Examination Guidelines for Computer Related Inventions which now read:

> Office personnel have had difficulty in properly treating claims directed to methods of doing business. Claims should not be categorized as methods of doing business. Instead such claims should be treated like any other process claims.

Examination Guidelines, 61 Fed.Reg. 7478, 7479 (1996). We agree that this is precisely the manner in which this type of claim should be treated. Whether the claims are directed to subject matter within § 101 should not turn on whether the claimed subject matter does "business" instead of something else.

CONCLUSION

The appealed decision is reversed and the case is remanded to the district court for further proceedings consistent with this opinion.

NOTES

Insert on page 600, in lieu of Notes 2 and 3:

2. *Computer Programs*. Because the mental-steps doctrine considered any series of steps that *could* be performed in a person's head unpatentable, it was clear from the dawn of the computer era that programs would pose problems to patent law. But surprisingly, the first Court to consider programs put its objection in more general terms. Thus, in Gottschalk v. Benson,[3] the issue was whether a computerized method for converting numerals expressed as binary-coded decimals into pure binary numerals was a patentable process. The Court held it was not. Justice Douglas explained:

> It is conceded that one may not patent an idea. But in practical effect, that would be the result if the formula for converting binary code to pure binary were patented in this case. The mathematical formula involved here has no substantial practical application except in connection with a digital computer, which means that if the judgment below is affirmed, the patent would wholly pre-empt the mathematical formula and in practical effect would be a patent on the algorithm itself.[4]

After the defeat in *Benson*, many patent applicants changed their strategy. Instead of applying for patents on mathematical manipulations, they tried to conform their claims to the process paradigm described by

[3] 409 U.S. 63, 93 S.Ct. 253, 34 L.Ed.2d 273 (1972).

[4] Id. at 71–72, 93 S.Ct. at 257. Justice Douglas defined "algorithm" as "[a] procedure for solving a given type of mathematical problem," id. at 65, 93 S.Ct. at 257.

Cochrane v. Deener. That tack was first reviewed by the Supreme Court in Parker v. Flook.[5] In that case, the claims were drawn to a physical reaction: the catalytic conversion of hydrocarbons. The process used a computer program to continuously monitor a set of variables, compare changes in the variables, and signal abnormalities so that the reaction could be stopped. Flook was careful to stress the chemical changes occurring in the course of using his program rather than focus on the operation of the program itself. Nonetheless, the Court held the claim unpatentable, saying that a "conventional, post-solution application" that was well known in the art could not turn a rule of nature into patentable subject matter.

Four years later, in Diamond v. Diehr,[6] the Court returned to the question, but this time it provided an answer more favorable to those who thought patent rights necessary to the continued vitality of the computer field. The invention at issue in *Diehr* was a process for curing rubber in a mold. The essentials of the process were commonly used in the rubber manufacturing industry, but it was not efficient as it was difficult to calculate when the rubber should be released from the mold. Diehr's solution coupled a standard device for measuring temperature to a computer programmed to use the well-known Arrhenius rate equation to continuously calculate the curing time from the temperature and signal when the curing process was finished. The Court found that:

> The "Arrhenius" equation is not patentable in isolation, but when a process for curing rubber is devised which incorporates in it a more efficient solution of the equation, that process is at the very least not barred at the threshold by § 101.[7]

Despite the promise *Diehr* held for computer patents, implementing its holding proved difficult. The striking similarity between the processes at issue in *Flook* and *Diehr*, coupled with *Diehr*'s failure to articulate a standard for drawing the elusive line between ideas and embodiments, spawned much confusion and, as *State Street Bank* shows, several lines of cases. The *Freeman-Walter Abele* analysis was the product of the Court of Claims and Patent Appeals (CCPA), which at the time of the first generation of computer cases was the court that reviewed PTO decisions. Based on the language in *Benson*, it attempted to decide whether any algorithms recited in a claim in fact preempted a principle of nature. The Court of Appeals for the Federal Circuit, which replaced the CCPA in 1982, continued to cite this test, but also looked for specific limitations. In In re Alappat,[8] the limiting embodiment was the machine that executes the program. In In re Grams,[9] the embodiment was the physical process that the program mediates. The entire process was considered patentable, but

[5] 437 U.S. 584, 98 S.Ct. 2522, 57 L.Ed.2d 451 (1978).

[6] 450 U.S. 175, 101 S.Ct. 1048, 67 L.Ed.2d 155 (1981).

[7] Id. at 188, 101 S.Ct. at 1057.

[8] 33 F.3d 1526 (Fed. Cir. 1994).

[9] 888 F.2d 835 (Fed. Cir. 1989).

only if it involved more than "mere" post-solution activity (the problem in *Flook*) or the gathering of data (the problem in *Grams*). Dissatisfaction with these efforts was, however, rampant. Right before the casebook went to press, the PTO released guidelines to help its examiners through the problems the cases presented. A summary appears on pages 603–604, but there is no point in reading it as the guidelines were withdrawn almost immediately on the ground that they were more confusing than helpful. The PTO later promulgated a revision, which can be found at its website, http://www.uspto.gov, but it is only a little less problematic.

In fact, many observers thought the problem was not in articulating a way to decide when a patent preempts a principle, but rather in *Benson* itself. Some thought Justice Douglas incorrect in assuming that algorithms always recite rules of nature. In their view, mathematical notation is just a form of language; it is sometimes used to express principles of nature, but not always. Sometimes math expresses thoughts that could be said, albeit at greater length, in English.[10] When that is the case, there is no problem in allowing the patent to protect all uses of the algorithm. Others arrived at the same conclusion by noting that even programs that are about rules of nature rarely utilize the actual principle. That is because principles of nature are too complicated to use in commercially significant applications; the inventive feature of most programs is the way the program simplifies the actual principle without losing its relevance to the problem at hand. In a concurring opinion to the *Arrhythmia* decision discussed in *State Street Bank*, Judge Rader had the following to say about the patentability of a program that analyzes electrocardiograph signals in order to determine certain characteristics of heart function in the hours immediately after a heart attack:

> While many . . . steps involve the mathematical manipulation of data, the claims do not describe a law of nature or a natural phenomenon. Furthermore the claims do not disclose mere abstract ideas, but a practical and potentially life-saving process. Regardless of whether performed by computer, these steps comprise a "process" within the meaning of § 101.[11]

It is against this backdrop that *State Street Bank* was handed down. How well does it deal with the problems that computer-implemented inventions have generated? Has the Federal Circuit now rejected *Benson*? See also AT & T Corp. v. Excel Communications, Inc.[12] The patent in that case, entitled "Call Message Recording for Telephone Systems," covers methodology that aids long-distance carriers in providing differential billing treatment for subscribers, depending upon whether a subscriber calls

---

[10] See, e.g., In re Meyer, 688 F.2d 789 (C.C.P.A. 1982).

[11] Arrhythmia Research Technology, Inc. v. Corazonix Corp., 958 F.2d 1053, 1060 (Fed. Cir. 1992).

[12] 172 F.3d 1352, 50 U.S.P.Q. 2d 1447 (Fed. Cir. 1999).

someone with the same or a different long-distance carrier. Although the process basically involves plugging data about subscribers' and call recipients' primary interchange carriers (PICs) into an algebraic formula that then produces a billing record, the court upheld the patent. As to *Benson*, the court reasoned:

> [The Court] never intended to create an overly broad, fourth category of [mathematical] subject matter excluded from § 101. Rather, at the core of the Court's analysis . . . lies an attempt by the Court to explain a rather straightforward concept, namely, that certain types of mathematical subject matter, standing alone, represent nothing more than abstract ideas until reduced to some type of practical application, and thus that subject matter is not, in and of itself, entitled to patent protection.

On Diehr, the court stated:

> The notion of "physical transformation" can be misunderstood. In the first place, it is not an invariable requirement, nut merely one example of how a mathematical algorithm may bring about a useful application.

How does the test articulated in *State Street Bank* and *AT & T* deal with the concern that fundamental relationships will become subject to private ownership? As we will see, claims drafted in "means plus function" form allow a patentee to assert as infringing devices and practices utilizing an equivalent of the means shown. Moreover, the patentee's right of action is not confined to literal infringement. As with copyright's substantial similarity test and trademark's confusing similarity test, patentees can assert rights against those who use "equivalents" of their inventions. See Assignment 22, Notes 2 and 7 in the casebook.

Is this the ideal resolution of the computer program problem? Remember, the real concern is protecting the public domain—making sure that patentees do not tie up every application of a principle of nature, including applications they have not invented. At least two other methods for achieving that result are possible, both of which are less abstract than the inquiry required by the subject-matter cases. First, applications could be rejected for failure to meet the specification requirements. As the Introductory Assignment explained, § 112 requires the patentee to give enough information in his specification to enable persons with skill in the art to practice the invention. Since as-yet-undiscovered applications will often not be enabled, overbroad claiming runs afoul of § 112. Second, instead of limiting the patentee during issuance, when future applications are difficult to predict, limitations could be imposed at the infringement stage. At that point, it is clear what other uses can be made of the principle the patentee claims to have invented. If he did not enable that application, the use should not be considered infringement.

3. *Business methods*. *State Street Bank* is clearly of considerable importance to the computer industry. However, its real significance is to the business sector. As we saw, one of the old rules of thumb held business

methods unpatentable. Although use of thumbs to decide abstract issues was long questionable, prior to the computer program cases, there was general agreement that business methods were not among the technologies at which patent law was directed. Once processes using programs became patentable, however, business methods that utilized programs were drawn into the fold. In Paine, Webber, Jackson & Curtis, Inc. v. Merrill, Lynch, Pierce, Fenner & Smith, Inc.,[13] for example, the court upheld the patent on a "Cash Management Account" that used a computer to track clients' deposits in a brokerage securities account, a money market fund, and a Visa charge/checking account.

State Street Bank arguably takes this approach one step further: by unequivocally rejecting the business method exception, it appears to make *all* business methods susceptible to patenting, even those that do not involve computers. Is this wise? Michael Milken made a fortune selling high risk bonds offering substantial interest. These "junk bonds" proved very popular in the market; many acquisitions have been financed with them. How much more would Milken have made had he been able to patent junk bonds or the process of using them to raise capital? Could the airline that first thought up frequent flyer miles have gained an even greater competitive advantage by patenting the practice of awarding them? How about protection for the tools of other professions: should sports moves—pitches, end-zone wiggles, high jumps—be patentable? Novel legal theories?[14]

Judge Rich rejected both the mathematical algorithm and business method exceptions on the ground that they are not supported by § 101. But the prohibitions on patenting laws of nature, natural phenomena, or abstract ideas are not found in the statute either. Important policies support these prohibitions: are there equally good reasons to leave business methods in the public domain, where all competitors can utilize them? Is the investment Milken made in convincing the market that junk bonds, though novel, are respectable investment vehicles, the kind of investment patent law is aimed at encouraging? Was the Supreme Court wise to deny *certiorari* in *State Street Bank*?[15]

Insert on page 607, in Note 4, after c.:

d. *Genetic and protein sequences.* The PTO is in the process of proposing new rules for claims involving nucleotide and amino-acid sequences. As with computer-related inventions, the best place to keep abreast of these changes is on the Patent and Trademark Office's website, see the insert into Note 2, supra.

---

[13] 564 F. Supp. 1358 (D.Del. 1983).

[14] See John R. Thomas, The Patenting of the Liberal Professions, 40 Boston College L. Rev. ___ (1999).

[15] See ___ U.S. ___, 119 S.Ct. 851, 142 L.Ed.2d 704 (1999).

Insert on page 608, after Note 5:

6. *Medical procedures*. Should a surgeon be permitted to patent a new type of incision? Should medical treatments be the subject of exclusive rights? After several patents on surgical methods were issued and enforced, Congress became concerned because these patents limited access to, and increased the price of, important medical methods. Moreover, there was no indication that physicians and surgeons needed a patent incentive to perfect their methods. In 1996, the decision was made to limit patent protection for medical procedures. However, for technical reasons, the subject matter provisions of the statute were not changed. Instead, § 287, the provision on damages limitations, was amended. Section 287(c)(1) now provides that a medical practitioner's performance of a medical activity that constitutes infringement cannot be the basis for monetary or injunctive relief against the medical practitioner or a health related care entity. These terms are defined in § 287(c)(2).

ASSIGNMENT 17

UTILITY

NOTES

Insert on page 623, after Note 6:

7. *Proving utility.* In general, the patent applicant does claim a utility. For most types of inventions, the PTO then simply assumes that the invention is operable for this recited purpose. In cases where the patent office can make a credible claim that the invention is not useful, the applicant is required to furnish further evidence, but the burden of proof is on the PTO to demonstrate that the invention is not useful. In cases involving human medications (where the term "patent medicine" has acquired somewhat of a bad name), however, more is required: the applicant must demonstrate that the assertion of utility is credible to a person with ordinary skill in the art. Usually, patent applications are filed long before the FDA has granted the applicant permission to use her invention on humans. Accordingly, this showing is made by analogy: the applicant demonstrates that the product is biologically active in a test tube or in animals and also shows that similar products with similar indicia of activity later did turn out to have therapeutic effect in humans. The person with ordinary skill is deemed to reason that if there is a correlation between animal and human activity for similar products, that same correlation will hold for the claimed product.

For most medicines, this system has worked well. However, when the products of biotechnology first came "on line" there was a problem. Since many of these products were meant to treat conditions that previously had no known treatment, there was no animal or test tube model with which to demonstrate utility. With no way to draw an analogy between what happened in animals or the test tube and what would happen in humans, the PTO rejected several such applications on utility grounds. According to the PTO, these inventors must wait until the completion of human testing to file patent applications. This practice generated considerable controversy and led the PTO to hold hearings on the utility problem. Several speakers testified that the failure to secure patents made it difficult for biotechnology start-up companies to attract investment capital, which, in turn, made it impossible to fund human testing. When it became clear that the new biotechnology industry was endangered by this vicious cycle (no patent without human tests, no money for human tests without a patent), the PTO quickly issued new guidelines which eased the burden of proving utility in these cases.[1]

BIBLIOGRAPHY

Insert on page 624, in the paragraph on genes:

Eisenberg & Merges, Opinion Letter as to the Patentability of Certain Inventions Associated With Identification of Partial cDNA Sequences, 23 AIPLA Q. J. 1 (1995).

[1] See PTO Utility Examination Guidelines, 60 Fed. Reg. 36,263 (1995). See also In re Brana, 51 F.3d 1560 (Fed.Cir.1995).

ASSIGNMENT 19

NONOBVIOUSNESS AND ORIGINALITY

NOTES

Insert on page 684, at the end of Note 4:

In fact, there may be quite a bit of room to maneuver. Although the CAFC does not appear willing to admit that *Durden* was wrong, it has retrenched even further. For example, in In re Ochiai,[1] the court was again faced with a question about the nonobviousness of a known process using and resulting in new compounds. The applicant had claimed a method for reacting a newly discovered (and patented) acid with other chemicals to produce a new member of the "cephem" family of compounds having antibiotic properties. The examiner and the Board rejected the process claim, claim 6, on *Durden* grounds. The CAFC reversed, stating:

"The process invention Ochiai recites in claim 6 specifically requires use of none other than its new, nonobvious acid as one of the starting materials. One having no knowledge of this acid could hardly find it obvious to make any cephem using this acid as an acylating agent, much less the particular cephem recited in claim 6.

* * *

"In addition, although the prior art references the examiner discussed do indeed teach the use of various acids to make various cephems, they do not define a class of acids the knowledge of which would render obvious the use of Ochiai's specifically claimed acid. The Board noted that Ochiai's specifically claimed acid is 'similar' to the acids used in the prior art. Likewise, the examiner asserted that the claimed acid was 'slightly different' from those taught in the cited references. Neither characterization, however, can establish the obviousness of the use of a starting material that is new and nonobvious, both in general and in the claimed process. The mere chemical possibility that one of those prior art acids could be modified such that its use would lead to the particular cephem recited in claim 6 does not make the process recited in claim 6 obvious 'unless the prior art suggested the desirability of [such a] modification.' In re Gordon, 733 F.2d 900, 902, 221 U.S.P.Q. 1125, 1127 (Fed.Cir.1984)."

[1] 71 F.3d 1565 (Fed.Cir.1995).

It now remains to be seen whether § 103(b) will ever be needed.

Insert on page 684, at the end of Note 5:

Issues concerning the presumption of validity generally arise in the course of litigating patentability in proceedings between private parties. A related question concerns the degree of deference that should be given to PTO fact finding.[2] The Federal Circuit had been using the "clearly erroneous" test, a stricter standard than the "arbitrary and capricious" and "unsupported by substantial evidence" tests set out in the Administrative Procedure Act, which governs the review of agency action generally.[3] In part, the court reasoned that the stricter standard was consonant with historical practice. And, since the PTO's decisions can be challenged in two ways—by direct review to the Federal Circuit or by filing an original action in the district court, the Federal Circuit also considered it necessary to examine PTO fact finding on the same standard used for reviewing lower court decisions.[4]

However, in a recent case, the Supreme Court disagreed. Dickinson v. Zurko[5] was a challenge to the PTO's denial of a patent on a method for increasing computer security. The Federal Circuit used the "clearly erroneous" test to set aside the factual findings underlying the determination of obviousness. The Supreme Court reversed, holding that the APA standard applied. After brushing aside the historical argument, the Court suggested that the anomaly created by reviewing district court decisions and PTO decisions on different standards could be handled by allowing the Federal Circuit to "adjust related review standards where necessary." Since the Supreme Court has not allowed the Federal Circuit to adjust reviewing standards in the past, this language is something of a surprise.[6] Moreover, the deference that will now be accorded to the PTO contrasts rather starkly with the way that the Court treated its decisions in the cases in this Assignment. Could it be that the Court was influenced by the fact that the PTO *denied* Zurko's patent, whereas the patents in *Graham* and *Sakraida* had both been *granted*? Will the Court come to regret its decision in *Zurko*? Or, will *Zurko* encourage the PTO to bring its practice in line with that of other administrative agencies?

Insert on page 686, after Note 7:

8. *The problem of secret prior art.* In addition to the problem of maintaining information flows within firms, which was solved by the last sentence of § 103(c), there are two other problems with rejecting applications on the basis of § 102(f)/103: first, these rejections blur the distinction between

---

[2] See 35 U.S.C. § 141.

[3] 5 U.S.C. § 706(2)(A) and (E).

[4] In re Zurko, 142 F.3d 1447 (Fed.Cir. 1998).

[5] __ U.S. __, 119 S.Ct. 1816, __ L.Ed.2d __ (1999).

[6] See Dennison Manufacturing Co. v. Panduit Corp., 475 U.S. 809, 106 S.Ct. 1578, 89 L.Ed.2d 817 (1986)(per curiam).

provisions that maintain the integrity of the public domain and provisions that insure that the patent is awarded to a true inventor; second, these rejections raise litigation costs. The distinction is blurred because information told only to an applicant is not really in the public domain. Since it is secret, the applicant accomplished *something* that no ordinary artisan could have done. Costs increase because the possibility of such a rejection creates incentives to investigate everything the applicant ever heard or saw, and require a court or the PTO to indulge in complicated determinations about the interaction between public material and information whose exact scope is uncertain. For this reason, some of the Federal Circuit judges have urged their colleagues to reconsider the propriety of these rejections.[7] However, when the issue recently came squarely before the court, it upheld § 102(f)/ 103 practice, albeit reluctantly. The case was OddzOn Products, Inc. v. Just Toys, Inc.,[8] which concerned a design patent on the "Vortex" ball, a foam football-like object with a tail and fin structure. Here is an excerpt from the decision:

The Prior Art Status of § 102(f) Subject Matter

The district court ruled that two confidential ball designs (the "disclosures") which "inspired" the inventor of the OddzOn design were prior art for purposes of determining obviousness under § 103. The district court noted that this court had recently declined to rule definitively on the relationship between § 102(f) and § 103, see Lamb–Weston, Inc. v. McCain Foods, Ltd., 78 F.3d 540, 544, 37 U.S.P.Q.2d 1856, 1858–59 (Fed.Cir.1996), but relied on the fact that the United States Patent and Trademark Office (PTO) interprets prior art under § 103 as including disclosures encompassed within § 102(f). OddzOn challenges the court's determination that subject matter encompassed within § 102(f) is prior art for purposes of an obviousness inquiry under § 103. OddzOn asserts that because these disclosures are not known to the public, they do not possess the usual hallmark of prior art, which is that they provide actual or constructive public knowledge. OddzOn argues that while the two disclosures constitute patent-defeating subject matter under 35 U.S.C. § 102(f), they cannot be combined with "real" prior art to defeat patentability under a combination of § 102(f) and § 103.

The prior art status under § 103 of subject matter derived by an applicant for patent within the meaning of § 102(f) has never expressly been decided by this court. We now take the opportunity to settle the persistent question whether § 102(f) is a prior art provision for purposes of § 103. As will be discussed, although there is a basis to suggest that § 102(f) should not be considered as a prior art provision, we hold that a

---

[7] See, e.g., Lamb–Weston Inc. v. McCain Foods Ltd, 78 F.3d 540, 546 (Fed. Cir. 1996)(Newman, J., dissenting); Gambro Lun-   dia AB v. Baxter Healthcare Corp., 110 F.3d 1573 (Fed. Cir. 1997).

[8] 122 F.3d 1396 (Fed. Cir. 1997).

fair reading of § 103, as amended in 1984, leads to the conclusion that § 102(f) is a prior art provision for purposes of § 103.

Section 102(f) provides that a person shall be entitled to a patent unless "he did not himself invent the subject matter sought to be patented." This is a derivation provision, which provides that one may not obtain a patent on that which is obtained from someone else whose possession of the subject matter is inherently "prior." It does not pertain only to public knowledge, but also applies to private communications between the inventor and another which may never become public. Subsections (a), (b), (e), and (g), on the other hand, are clearly prior art provisions. They relate to knowledge manifested by acts that are essentially public. Subsections (a) and (b) relate to public knowledge or use, or prior patents and printed publications; subsection (e) relates to prior filed applications for patents of others which have become public by grant; and subsection (g) relates to prior inventions of others that are either public or will likely become public in the sense that they have not been abandoned, suppressed, or concealed. Subsections (c) and (d) are loss-of-right provisions. Section 102(c) precludes the obtaining of a patent by inventors who have abandoned their invention. Section 102(d) causes an inventor to lose the right to a patent by delaying the filing of a patent application too long after having filed a corresponding patent application in a foreign country. Subsections (c) and (d) are therefore not prior art provisions.

In In re Bass, 59 C.C.P.A. 1342, 474 F.2d 1276, 1290, 177 U.S.P.Q. 178, 189 (CCPA 1973), the principal opinion of the Court of Customs and Patent Appeals held that a prior invention of another that was not abandoned, suppressed, or concealed (102(g) prior art) could be combined with other prior art to support rejection of a claim for obviousness under § 103. The principal opinion noted that the provisions of § 102 deal with two types of issues, those of novelty and loss-of-right. It explained: "Three of [the subsections,] (a), (e), and (g), deal with events prior to applicant's invention date and the other, (b), with events more than one year prior to the U.S. application date. These are the 'prior art' subsections." Id. The principal opinion added, in dictum (§ 102(f) not being at issue), that "[o]f course, (c), (d), and (f) have no relation to § 103 and no relevancy to what is 'prior art' under § 103." Id. There is substantial logic to that conclusion. After all, the other prior art provisions all relate to subject matter that is, or eventually becomes, public. Even the "secret prior art" of § 102(e) is ultimately public in the form of an issued patent before it attains prior art status.

Thus, the patent laws have not generally recognized as prior art that which is not accessible to the public. It has been a basic principle of patent law, subject to minor exceptions, that prior art is:

> technology already available to the public. It is available, in legal theory at least, when it is described in the world's accessible literature, including patents, or has been publicly known or in . . . public use or on sale "in this country." That is the real meaning of "prior art" in legal theory—it is knowledge that is available, including what would be obvious from it, at a given time, to a person of ordinary skill in the art.

Kimberly–Clark Corp. v. Johnson & Johnson, 745 F.2d 1437, 1453, 223 U.S.P.Q. 603, 614 (Fed.Cir.1984) (citations omitted).

Moreover, as between an earlier inventor who has not given the public the benefit of the invention, e.g., because the invention has been abandoned without public disclosure, suppressed, or concealed, and a subsequent inventor who obtains a patent, the policy of the law is for the subsequent inventor to prevail. See W.L. Gore & Assocs., Inc. v. Garlock, Inc., 721 F.2d 1540, 1550, 220 U.S.P.Q. 303, 310 (Fed.Cir.1983) ("Early public disclosure is a linchpin of the patent system. As between a prior inventor [who does not disclose] and a later inventor who promptly files a patent application . . ., the law favors the latter."). Likewise, when the possessor of secret art (art that has been abandoned, suppressed, or concealed) that predates the critical date is faced with a later-filed patent, the later-filed patent should not be invalidated in the face of this "prior" art, which has not been made available to the public. Thus, prior, but non-public, inventors yield to later inventors who utilize the patent system.

However, a change occurred in the law after Bass was decided. At the time Bass was decided, § 103 read as follows:

> A patent may not be obtained though the invention is not identically disclosed or described as set forth in section 102 of this title, if the differences between the subject matter sought to be patented and the prior art are such that the subject matter as a whole would have been obvious at the time the invention was made to a person having ordinary skill in the art to which said subject matter pertains. Patentability shall not be negatived by the manner in which the invention was made.

35 U.S.C. § 103. The prior art being referred to in that provision arguably included only public prior art defined in subsections 102(a), (b), (e), and (g).

In 1984, Congress amended § 103, adding the following paragraph:

> Subject matter developed by another person, which qualifies as prior art only under subsection (f) or (g) of section 102 of this title, shall not preclude patentability under this section where the subject matter and the claimed invention were, at the time the invention was made, owned by the same person or subject to an obligation of assignment to the same person.

35 U.S.C. § 103 (now § 103(c)). It is historically very clear that this provision was intended to avoid the invalidation of patents under § 103 on the basis of the work of fellow employees engaged in team research. See Section-by-Section Analysis: Patent Law Amendments Act of 1984, 130 Cong. Rec. 28069, 28071 (Oct. 1, 1984), reprinted in 1984 U.S.C.C.A.N. 5827, 5833 (stating that the amendment, which encourages communication among members of research teams, was a response to Bass and In re Clemens, 622 F.2d 1029, 206 U.S.P.Q. 289 (CCPA 1980), in which "an earlier invention which is not public may be treated under Section 102(g), and possibly under 102(f), as prior art"). There was no clearly apparent purpose in Congress's inclusion of § 102(f) in the amendment other than an attempt to ameliorate the problems of patenting the results of team research. However, the language appears in the statute; it was enacted by Congress. We must give effect to it.

The statutory language provides a clear statement that subject matter that qualifies as prior art under subsection (f) or (g) cannot be combined with other prior art to render a claimed invention obvious and hence unpatentable when the relevant prior art is commonly owned with the claimed invention at the time the invention was made. While the statute does not expressly state in so many words that § 102(f) creates a type of prior art for purposes of § 103, nonetheless that conclusion is inescapable; the language that states that § 102(f) subject matter is not prior art under limited circumstances clearly implies that it is prior art otherwise. That is what Congress wrote into law in 1984 and that is the way we must read the statute.

This result is not illogical. It means that an invention, A', that is obvious in view of subject matter A, derived from another, is also unpatentable. The obvious invention, A', may not be unpatentable to the inventor of A, and it may not be unpatentable to a third party who did not receive the disclosure of A, but it is unpatentable to the party who did receive the disclosure.

The PTO's regulations also adopt this interpretation of the statute. 37 C.F.R. § 1.106(d) (1996) ("Subject matter which is developed by another person which qualifies as prior art only under 35 U.S.C. § 102(f) or (g) may be used as prior art under 35 U.S.C. § 103."). Although the PTO's interpretation of this statute is not conclusive, we agree with the district court that it is a reasonable interpretation of the statute.

It is sometimes more important that a close question be settled one way or another than which way it is settled. We settle the issue here (subject of course to any later intervention by Congress or review by the Supreme Court), and do so in a manner that best comports with the voice of Congress. Thus, while there is a basis for an opposite conclusion, principally based on the fact that § 102(f) does not refer to public activity, as do the other provisions that clearly define prior art, nonetheless we cannot escape the import of the 1984 amendment. We therefore hold that subject matter derived from another not only is itself unpatentable to the party who derived it under § 102(f), but, when combined with other prior art, may make a resulting obvious invention unpatentable to that party under a combination of §§ 102(f) and 103. Accordingly, the district court did not err by considering the two design disclosures known to the inventor to be prior art under the combination of §§ 102(f) and 103.[9]

BIBLIOGRAPHY

Insert on page 686:

Eisenberg & Merges, Opinion Letter as to the Patentability of Certain Inventions Associated With Identification of Partial cDNA Sequences, 23 AIPLA Q. J. 1 (1995).

[9] Id. at 1401–1404.

ASSIGNMENT 20

STATUTORY BARS

Insert on page 693, in lieu of *UMC Electronics*:

Pfaff Electronics Co. v. Well Electronics, Inc.

Supreme Court of the United States, 1998.
___ U.S. ___, 119 S.Ct. 304, 142 L.Ed.2d 261.

■ JUSTICE STEVENS delivered the opinion of the Court.

Section 102(b) of the Patent Act of 1952 provides that no person is entitled to patent an "invention" that has been "on sale" more than one year before filing a patent application. We granted certiorari to determine whether the commercial marketing of a newly invented product may mark the beginning of the 1–year period even though the invention has not yet been reduced to practice.

I

On April 19, 1982, petitioner, Wayne Pfaff, filed an application for a patent on a computer chip socket. Therefore, April 19, 1981, constitutes the critical date for purposes of the on-sale bar of 35 U.S.C. § 102(b); if the 1–year period began to run before that date, Pfaff lost his right to patent his invention.

Pfaff commenced work on the socket in November 1980, when representatives of Texas Instruments asked him to develop a new device for mounting and removing semiconductor chip carriers. In response to this request, he prepared detailed engineering drawings that described the design, the dimensions, and the materials to be used in making the socket. Pfaff sent those drawings to a manufacturer in February or March 1981.

Prior to March 17, 1981, Pfaff showed a sketch of his concept to representatives of Texas Instruments. On April 8, 1981, they provided Pfaff with a written confirmation of a previously placed oral purchase order for 30,100 of his new sockets for a total price of $91,155. In accord with his normal practice, Pfaff did not make and test a prototype of the new device before offering to sell it in commercial quantities.[1] The manufacturer took

---

[1] At his deposition, respondent's counsel engaged in the following colloquy with Pfaff:

"Q. Now, at this time [late 1980 or early 1981] did we [sic] have any prototypes

several months to develop the customized tooling necessary to produce the device, and Pfaff did not fill the order until July 1981. The evidence therefore indicates that Pfaff first reduced his invention to practice in the summer of 1981. The socket achieved substantial commercial success before Patent No. 4,491,377 (the '377 patent) issued to Pfaff on January 1, 1985.[2]

After the patent issued, petitioner brought an infringement action against respondent, Wells Electronics, Inc., the manufacturer of a competing socket. Wells prevailed on the basis of a finding of no infringement. When respondent began to market a modified device, petitioner brought this suit, alleging that the modifications infringed six of the claims in the § 377 patent. [The District Court held two claims invalid and upheld the rest, rejecting a defense based on § 102(b). The Court of Appeals reversed. It held two claims invalid on § 103 grounds and four claims invalid on § 102(b) grounds.] The conclusion [regarding § 102(b)] rested on the court's view that as long as the invention was "substantially complete at the time of sale," the 1–year period began to run, even though the invention had not yet been reduced to practice.

Because other courts have held or assumed that an invention cannot be "on sale" within the meaning of § 102(b) unless and until it has been reduced to practice, see, e.g., Timely Products Corp. v. Arron, 523 F.2d 288, 299–302 (C.A.2 1975); Dart Industries, Inc. v. E.I. du Pont De Nemours & Co., 489 F.2d 1359, 1365, n. 11 (C.A.7 1973), cert. denied, 417 U.S. 933, 94 S.Ct. 2645, 41 L.Ed.2d 236 (1974), and because the text of § 102(b) makes no reference to "substantial completion" of an invention, we granted certiorari. 523 U.S. ___, 118 S.Ct. 1183, 140 L.Ed.2d 315 (1998).

II

The primary meaning of the word "invention" in the Patent Act unquestionably refers to the inventor's conception rather than to a physical embodiment of that idea. The statute does not contain any express requirement that an invention must be reduced to practice before it can be patented. Neither the statutory definition of the term in § 100 nor the

developed or anything of that nature, working embodiment?

"A. No.

"Q. It was in a drawing. Is that correct?

"A. Strictly in a drawing. Went from the drawing to the hard tooling. That's the way I do my business.

"Q. 'Boom-boom'?

"A. You got it.

"Q. You are satisfied, obviously, when you come up with some drawings that it is going to go—'it works'?

"A. I know what I'm doing, yes, most of the time." App. 96–97.

[2] Initial sales of the patented device were:

1981	$ 350,000
1982	$ 937,000
1983	$2,800,000
1984	$3,430,000

App. to Pet. for Cert. 223.

basic conditions for obtaining a patent set forth in § 101 make any mention of "reduction to practice." The statute's only specific reference to that term is found in § 102(g), which sets forth the standard for resolving priority contests between two competing claimants to a patent. That subsection provides:

> "In determining priority of invention there shall be considered not only the respective dates of conception and reduction to practice of the invention, but also the reasonable diligence of one who was first to conceive and last to reduce to practice, from a time prior to conception by the other."

Thus, assuming diligence on the part of the applicant, it is normally the first inventor to conceive, rather than the first to reduce to practice, who establishes the right to the patent.

It is well settled that an invention may be patented before it is reduced to practice. In 1888, this Court upheld a patent issued to Alexander Graham Bell even though he had filed his application before constructing a working telephone. Chief Justice Waite's reasoning in that case merits quoting at length:

> "It is quite true that when Bell applied for his patent he had never actually transmitted telegraphically spoken words so that they could be distinctly heard and understood at the receiving end of his line, but in his specification he did describe accurately and with admirable clearness his process, that is to say, the exact electrical condition that must be created to accomplish his purpose, and he also described, with sufficient precision to enable one of ordinary skill in such matters to make it, a form of apparatus which, if used in the way pointed out, would produce the required effect, receive the words, and carry them to and deliver them at the appointed place. The particular instrument which he had, and which he used in his experiments, did not, under the circumstances in which it was tried, reproduce the words spoken, so that they could be clearly understood, but the proof is abundant and of the most convincing character, that other instruments, carefully constructed and made exactly in accordance with the specification, without any additions whatever, have operated and will operate successfully. A good mechanic of proper skill in matters of the kind can take the patent and, by following the specification strictly, can, without more, construct an apparatus which, when used in the way pointed out, will do all that it is claimed the method or process will do. . . .

> "The law does not require that a discoverer or inventor, in order to get a patent for a process, must have succeeded in bringing his art to the highest degree of perfection. It is enough if he describes his method with sufficient clearness and precision to enable those skilled in the matter to understand what the process is, and if he points out some practicable way of putting it into operation." The Telephone Cases, 126 U.S. 1, 535–536, 8 S.Ct. 778, 31 L.Ed. 863 (1888).[3]

---

[3] This Court has also held a patent invalid because the invention had previously been disclosed in a prior patent application, although that application did not claim the invention and the first invention apparently had not been reduced to practice. Alexander

When we apply the reasoning of The Telephone Cases to the facts of the case before us today, it is evident that Pfaff could have obtained a patent on his novel socket when he accepted the purchase order from Texas Instruments for 30,100 units. At that time he provided the manufacturer with a description and drawings that had "sufficient clearness and precision to enable those skilled in the matter" to produce the device. The parties agree that the sockets manufactured to fill that order embody Pfaff's conception as set forth in claims 1, 6, 7, and 10 of the '377 patent. We can find no basis in the text of § 102(b) or in the facts of this case for concluding that Pfaff's invention was not "on sale" within the meaning of the statute until after it had been reduced to practice.

III

Pfaff nevertheless argues that longstanding precedent, buttressed by the strong interest in providing inventors with a clear standard identifying the onset of the 1–year period, justifies a special interpretation of the word "invention" as used in § 102(b). We are persuaded that this nontextual argument should be rejected.

As we have often explained, most recently in Bonito Boats, Inc. v. Thunder Craft Boats, Inc., 489 U.S. 141, 151, 109 S.Ct. 971, 103 L.Ed.2d 118 (1989), the patent system represents a carefully crafted bargain that encourages both the creation and the public disclosure of new and useful advances in technology, in return for an exclusive monopoly for a limited period of time. The balance between the interest in motivating innovation and enlightenment by rewarding invention with patent protection on the one hand, and the interest in avoiding monopolies that unnecessarily stifle competition on the other, has been a feature of the federal patent laws since their inception.

Consistent with these ends, § 102 of the Patent Act serves as a limiting provision, both excluding ideas that are in the public domain from patent protection and confining the duration of the monopoly to the statutory term. See, e.g., Frantz Mfg. Co. v. Phenix Mfg. Co., 457 F.2d 314, 320 (C.A.7 1972).

We originally held that an inventor loses his right to a patent if he puts his invention into public use before filing a patent application. "His voluntary act or acquiescence in the public sale and use is an abandonment of his right" Pennock v. Dialogue, 2 Pet. 1, 24, 7 L.Ed. 327 (1829) (Story, J.). A similar reluctance to allow an inventor to remove existing knowledge from public use undergirds the on-sale bar.

Nevertheless, an inventor who seeks to perfect his discovery may conduct extensive testing without losing his right to obtain a patent for his

Milburn Co. v. Davis-Bournonville Co., 270 U.S. 390, 401–402, 46 S.Ct. 324, 70 L.Ed. 651 (1926).

invention—even if such testing occurs in the public eye. The law has long recognized the distinction between inventions put to experimental use and products sold commercially. In 1878, we explained why patentability may turn on an inventor's use of his product.

> "It is sometimes said that an inventor acquires an undue advantage over the public by delaying to take out a patent, inasmuch as he thereby preserves the monopoly to himself for a longer period than is allowed by the policy of the law; but this cannot be said with justice when the delay is occasioned by a bona fide effort to bring his invention to perfection, or to ascertain whether it will answer the purpose intended. His monopoly only continues for the allotted period, in any event; and it is the interest of the public, as well as himself, that the invention should be perfect and properly tested, before a patent is granted for it. Any attempt to use it for a profit, and not by way of experiment, for a longer period than two years before the application, would deprive the inventor of his right to a patent." Elizabeth v. American Nicholson Pavement Co., 97 U.S. 126, 137, 24 L.Ed. 1000 (1877) (emphasis added).

The patent laws therefore seek both to protect the public's right to retain knowledge already in the public domain and the inventor's right to control whether and when he may patent his invention. The Patent Act of 1836, 5 Stat. 117, was the first statute that expressly included an on-sale bar to the issuance of a patent. Like the earlier holding in Pennock, that provision precluded patentability if the invention had been placed on sale at any time before the patent application was filed. In 1839, Congress ameliorated that requirement by enacting a 2–year grace period in which the inventor could file an application. 5 Stat. 353.

In Andrews v. Hovey, 123 U.S. 267, 274, 8 S.Ct. 101, 31 L.Ed. 160 (1887), we noted that the purpose of that amendment was "to fix a period of limitation which should be certain"; it required the inventor to make sure that a patent application was filed "within two years from the completion of his invention," ibid. In 1939, Congress reduced the grace period from two years to one year. 53 Stat. 1212.

Petitioner correctly argues that these provisions identify an interest in providing inventors with a definite standard for determining when a patent application must be filed. A rule that makes the timeliness of an application depend on the date when an invention is "substantially complete" seriously undermines the interest in certainty.[4] Moreover, such a rule finds no

---

[4] The Federal Circuit has developed a multifactor, "totality of the circumstances" test to determine the trigger for the on-sale bar. See, e.g., Micro Chemical, Inc. v. Great Plains Chemical Co., 103 F.3d 1538, 1544 (C.A.Fed.1997) (stating that, in determining whether an invention is on sale for purposes of 102(b), " 'all of the circumstances surrounding the sale or offer to sell, including the stage of development of the invention and the nature of the invention, must be considered and weighed against the policies underlying section 102(b)' "); see also UMC Electronics Co. v. United States, 816 F.2d 647, 656 (1987) (stating the on-sale bar "does not lend itself to formulation into a set of precise requirements"). As the Federal Circuit itself has noted, this test "has been criticized as

support in the text of the statute. Thus, petitioner's argument calls into question the standard applied by the Court of Appeals, but it does not persuade us that it is necessary to engraft a reduction to practice element into the meaning of the term "invention" as used in § 102(b).

The word "invention" must refer to a concept that is complete, rather than merely one that is "substantially complete." It is true that reduction to practice ordinarily provides the best evidence that an invention is complete. But just because reduction to practice is sufficient evidence of completion, it does not follow that proof of reduction to practice is necessary in every case. Indeed, both the facts of the Telephone Cases and the facts of this case demonstrate that one can prove that an invention is complete and ready for patenting before it has actually been reduced to practice.

We conclude, therefore, that the on-sale bar applies when two conditions are satisfied before the critical date. First, the product must be the subject of a commercial offer for sale. An inventor can both understand and control the timing of the first commercial marketing of his invention. The experimental use doctrine, for example, has not generated concerns about indefiniteness, and we perceive no reason why unmanageable uncertainty should attend a rule that measures the application of the on-sale bar of § 102(b) against the date when an invention that is ready for patenting is first marketed commercially. In this case the acceptance of the purchase order prior to April 8, 1981, makes it clear that such an offer had been made, and there is no question that the sale was commercial rather than experimental in character.

Second, the invention must be ready for patenting. That condition may be satisfied in at least two ways: by proof of reduction to practice before the critical date; or by proof that prior to the critical date the inventor had prepared drawings or other descriptions of the invention that were sufficiently specific to enable a person skilled in the art to practice the invention. In this case the second condition of the on-sale bar is satisfied because the drawings Pfaff sent to the manufacturer before the critical date fully disclosed the invention.

The evidence in this case thus fulfills the two essential conditions of the on-sale bar. As succinctly stated by Learned Hand:

> "[I]t is a condition upon an inventor's right to a patent that he shall not exploit his discovery competitively after it is ready for patenting; he must content himself with either secrecy, or legal monopoly." Metallizing Engineering Co. v. Kenyon Bearing & Auto Parts Co., 153 F.2d 516, 520 (C.A.2 1946).

unnecessarily vague." Seal–Flex, Inc. v. Athletic Track & Court Construction, 98 F.3d 1318, 1323, n. 2 (C.A.Fed.1996).

The judgment of the Court of Appeals finds support not only in the text of the statute but also in the basic policies underlying the statutory scheme, including § 102(b). When Pfaff accepted the purchase order for his new sockets prior to April 8, 1981, his invention was ready for patenting. The fact that the manufacturer was able to produce the socket using his detailed drawings and specifications demonstrates this fact. Furthermore, those sockets contained all the elements of the invention claimed in the '377 patent. Therefore, Pfaff's '377 patent is invalid because the invention had been on sale for more than one year in this country before he filed his patent application. Accordingly, the judgment of the Court of Appeals is affirmed.

NOTES

Insert on page 708, at the end of Note 2:

For another case affirming the relevance of third-party art, see Evans Cooling System Inc. v. General Motors Corp.[5]

Insert on page 710, in lieu of Note 5 b:

b. Section 102(d). Section 102(d) is aimed at encouraging foreign inventors to patent their inventions in the United States. It is difficult to apply for protection in several countries simultaneously. Each country examines applications under its own law, charges a fee, and many will review only applications written in the official language of the country. Compliance is costly, and the applicant may not want to incur these costs until commercial value is assured. At the same time, the United States created patent law in order to encourage dissemination of advances to its own citizens. Inventors who disseminate only abroad are ignoring this interest and may even put the United States in a competitively inferior position.

Section 102(d) attempts to find a comfortable middle position between forcing people to invest in a U.S. patent before they are ready and allowing them to impose on Americans the costs of delay. It bars a patent on an invention for which a patent was applied for abroad under the authority of the U.S. applicant, but only if the foreign application is filed more than a year before the U.S. application is filed and only in the event that the foreign patent issues before the U.S. patent filing. In other words, two things are required to trigger § 102(d): first, a foreign filing more than a year before the U.S. filing; second, foreign issuance before U.S. filing.

Why is § 102(d) used infrequently? First, the bar is easy to avoid. All one has to do is file in the U.S. within a year of the foreign filing. Moreover, delays in foreign patent offices are as rampant as delays in the PTO. Unless the foreign application is filed a very long time before the U.S. application, it is not likely to issue before the applicant is ready to file in the United

---

[5] 125 F.3d 1448 (Fed. Cir. 1997).

States. Finally, § 102(d) is generally interpreted as requiring that the U.S. and foreign applications claim identical inventions.[6] The occasional applicant who misses the filing date may be able to avoid subsection (d) by carefully drafting the U.S. claims so they are not identical to the foreign claims.

[6] See, e.g., General Electric Co. v. Alexander, 280 F. 852 (2d Cir.1922)(decided under the predecessor of § 102(d)).

ASSIGNMENT 22

THE SCOPE OF THE PATENT HOLDER'S RIGHTS: INFRINGEMENT AND CONTRIBUTORY INFRINGEMENT

1. INTRODUCTION

Insert on page 734, in lieu of the first paragraph:

The Patent Act does not provide the patentee with any affirmative rights, such as to sell or license her invention. Rather, the Act gives to the patentee only the right to exclude others: a cause of action against those who make, use, sell, offer for sale, or import the patented invention in (or into) the United States. In addition to this action for infringement, the patentee can also recover from anyone who induces or contributes to infringement by others in the United States, imports into the United States products made abroad using a patented process, or distributes components for the assembly of a patented product abroad.

3. MATERIALS FOR SOLUTION OF PRINCIPAL PROBLEM

B. CASES:

Insert on page 744, after *Graver Tank & Manufacturing Co.*:

Warner–Jenkinson Company, Inc., v. Hilton Davis Chemical Co.

Supreme Court of the United States, 1997.
520 U.S. 17, 117 S.Ct. 1040, 137 L.Ed.2d 146.

■ JUSTICE THOMAS delivered the opinion of the Court.

Nearly 50 years ago, this Court in Graver Tank & Mfg. Co. v. Linde Air Products Co., 339 U.S. 605, 70 S.Ct. 854, 94 L.Ed. 1097 (1950), set out the modern contours of what is known in patent law as the "doctrine of equivalents." Under this doctrine, a product or process that does not literally infringe upon the express terms of a patent claim may nonetheless be found to infringe if there is "equivalence" between the elements of the accused product or process and the claimed elements of the patented invention. Id., at 609, 70 S.Ct., at 856–857. Petitioner, which was found to

100

have infringed upon respondent's patent under the doctrine of equivalents, invites us to speak the death of that doctrine. We decline that invitation. The significant disagreement within the Court of Appeals for the Federal Circuit concerning the application of Graver Tank suggests, however, that the doctrine is not free from confusion. We therefore will endeavor to clarify the proper scope of the doctrine.

I

The essential facts of this case are few. Petitioner Warner–Jenkinson Co. and respondent Hilton Davis Chemical Co. manufacture dyes. Impurities in those dyes must be removed. Hilton Davis holds United States Patent No. 4,560,746 ('746 patent), which discloses an improved purification process involving "ultrafiltration." The '746 process filters impure dye through a porous membrane at certain pressures and pH levels,[1] resulting in a high purity dye product.

The '746 patent issued in 1985. As relevant to this case, the patent claims as its invention an improvement in the ultrafiltration process as follows:

> "In a process for the purification of a dye ... the improvement which comprises: subjecting an aqueous solution ... to ultrafiltration through a membrane having a nominal pore diameter of 5–15 Angstroms under a hydrostatic pressure of approximately 200 to 400 p.s.i.g., *at a pH from approximately 6.0 to 9.0*, to thereby cause separation of said impurities from said dye...." App. 36–37 (emphasis added).

The inventors added the phrase "at a pH from approximately 6.0 to 9.0" during patent prosecution. At a minimum, this phrase was added to distinguish a previous patent (the "Booth" patent) that disclosed an ultrafiltration process operating at a pH above 9.0. The parties disagree as to why the low-end pH limit of 6.0 was included as part of the claim.[2]

In 1986, Warner–Jenkinson developed an ultrafiltration process that operated with membrane pore diameters assumed to be 5–15 Angstroms, at pressures of 200 to nearly 500 p.s.i.g., and at a pH of 5.0. Warner–

---

[1] The pH, or power (exponent) of Hydrogen, of a solution is a measure of its acidity or alkalinity. A pH of 7.0 is neutral; a pH below 7.0 is acidic; and a pH above 7.0 is alkaline. Although measurement of pH is on a logarithmic scale, with each whole number difference representing a ten-fold difference in acidity, the practical significance of any such difference will often depend on the context. Pure water, for example, has a neutral pH of 7.0, whereas carbonated water has an acidic pH of 3.0, and concentrated hydrochloric acid has a pH approaching 0.0. On the other end of the scale, milk of magnesia has a pH of 10.0, whereas household ammonia has a pH of 11.9. 21 Encyclopedia Americana 844 (Int'l ed.1990).

[2] Petitioner contends that the lower limit was added because below a pH of 6.0 the patented process created "foaming" problems in the plant and because the process was not shown to work below that pH level. Brief for Petitioner 4, n. 5, 37, n. 28. Respondent counters that the process was successfully tested to pH levels as low as 2.2 with no effect on the process because of foaming, but offers no particular explanation as to why the lower level of 6.0 pH was selected. Brief for Respondent 34, n. 34.

Jenkinson did not learn of the '746 patent until after it had begun commercial use of its ultrafiltration process. Hilton Davis eventually learned of Warner–Jenkinson's use of ultrafiltration and, in 1991, sued Warner–Jenkinson for patent infringement.

As trial approached, Hilton Davis conceded that there was no literal infringement, and relied solely on the doctrine of equivalents. Over Warner-Jenkinson's objection that the doctrine of equivalents was an equitable doctrine to be applied by the court, the issue of equivalence was included among those sent to the jury. The jury found that the '746 patent was not invalid and that Warner–Jenkinson infringed upon the patent under the doctrine of equivalents. The jury also found, however, that Warner–Jenkinson had not intentionally infringed, and therefore awarded only 20% of the damages sought by Hilton Davis. The District Court denied Warner–Jenkinson's post-trial motions, and entered a permanent injunction prohibiting Warner–Jenkinson from practicing ultrafiltration below 500 p.s.i.g. and below 9.01 pH. A fractured en banc Court of Appeals for the Federal Circuit affirmed. 62 F.3d 1512 (C.A.Fed.1995).

The majority below held that the doctrine of equivalents continues to exist and that its touchstone is whether substantial differences exist between the accused process and the patented process. Id., at 1521–1522. The court also held that the question of equivalence is for the jury to decide and that the jury in this case had substantial evidence from which it could conclude that the Warner–Jenkinson process was not substantially different from the ultrafiltration process disclosed in the '746 patent. Id., at 1525.

There were three separate dissents, commanding a total of 5 of 12 judges. Four of the five dissenting judges viewed the doctrine of equivalents as allowing an improper expansion of claim scope, contrary to this Court's numerous holdings that it is the claim that defines the invention and gives notice to the public of the limits of the patent monopoly. Id., at 1537–1538 (Plager, J., dissenting). The fifth dissenter, the late Judge Nies, was able to reconcile the prohibition against enlarging the scope of claims and the doctrine of equivalents by applying the doctrine to each element of a claim, rather than to the accused product or process "overall." Id., at 1574 (Nies, J., dissenting). As she explained it, "[t]he 'scope' is not enlarged if courts do not go beyond the substitution of equivalent elements." Ibid. All of the dissenters, however, would have found that a much narrowed doctrine of equivalents may be applied in whole or in part by the court. Id., at 1540–1542 (Plager, J., dissenting); id., at 1579 (Nies, J., dissenting).

We granted certiorari, 516 U.S. ___, 116 S.Ct. 1014, 134 L.Ed.2d 95 (1996), and now reverse and remand.

II

In Graver Tank we considered the application of the doctrine of equivalents to an accused chemical composition for use in welding that differed from the patented welding material by the substitution of one chemical element. 339 U.S., at 610, 70 S.Ct., at 857. The substituted element did not fall within the literal terms of the patent claim, but the Court nonetheless found that the "question which thus emerges is whether the substitution [of one element for the other] . . . is a change of such substance as to make the doctrine of equivalents inapplicable; or conversely, whether under the circumstances the change was so insubstantial that the trial court's invocation of the doctrine of equivalents was justified." Ibid. The Court also described some of the considerations that go into applying the doctrine of equivalents:

> "What constitutes equivalency must be determined against the context of the patent, the prior art, and the particular circumstances of the case. Equivalence, in the patent law, is not the prisoner of a formula and is not an absolute to be considered in a vacuum. It does not require complete identity for every purpose and in every respect. In determining equivalents, things equal to the same thing may not be equal to each other and, by the same token, things for most purposes different may sometimes be equivalents. Consideration must be given to the purpose for which an ingredient is used in a patent, the qualities it has when combined with the other ingredients, and the function which it is intended to perform. An important factor is whether persons reasonably skilled in the art would have known of the interchangeability of an ingredient not contained in the patent with one that was." Id., at 609, 70 S.Ct., at 856–857.

Considering those factors, the Court viewed the difference between the chemical element claimed in the patent and the substitute element to be "colorable only," and concluded that the trial court's judgment of infringement under the doctrine of equivalents was proper. Id., at 612, 70 S.Ct., at 858.

A

Petitioner's primary argument in this Court is that the doctrine of equivalents, as set out in Graver Tank in 1950, did not survive the 1952 revision of the Patent Act, 35 U.S.C. § 100 et seq., because it is inconsistent with several aspects of that Act. In particular, petitioner argues: (1) the doctrine of equivalents is inconsistent with the statutory requirement that a patentee specifically "claim" the invention covered by a patent, 35 U.S.C. § 112; (2) the doctrine circumvents the patent reissue process— designed to correct mistakes in drafting or the like—and avoids the express limitations on that process, 35 U.S.C. §§ 251–252; (3) the doctrine is inconsistent with the primacy of the Patent and Trademark Office (PTO) in setting the scope of a patent through the patent prosecution process; and (4) the doctrine was implicitly rejected as a general matter by Congress' specific and limited inclusion of the doctrine in one section regarding "means" claiming, 35 U.S.C. § 112, ¶ 6. All but one of these arguments were made in Graver Tank in the context of the 1870 Patent Act, and failed to command a majority.[3]

The 1952 Patent Act is not materially different from the 1870 Act with regard to claiming, reissue, and the role of the PTO. Compare, e.g., 35 U.S.C. § 112 ("The specification shall conclude with one or more claims particularly pointing out and distinctly claiming the subject matter which the applicant regards as his invention") with The Consolidated Patent Act of 1870, ch. 230, § 26, 16 Stat. 198, 201 (the applicant "shall particularly point out and distinctly claim the part, improvement, or combination which he claims as his invention or discovery"). Such minor differences as exist between those provisions in the 1870 and the 1952 Acts have no bearing on the result reached in Graver Tank, and thus provide no basis for our overruling it. In the context of infringement, we have already held that pre–1952 precedent survived the passage of the 1952 Act. See Aro Mfg. Co. v. Convertible Top Replacement Co., 365 U.S. 336, 342, 81 S.Ct. 599, 602–603, 5 L.Ed.2d 592 (1961) (new section defining infringement "left intact the entire body of case law on direct infringement"). We see no reason to reach a different result here.[4]

Petitioner's fourth argument for an implied congressional negation of the doctrine of equivalents turns on the reference to "equivalents" in the "means" claiming provision of the 1952 Act. Section 112, ¶ 6, a provision not contained in the 1870 Act, states:

> "An element in a claim for a combination may be expressed as a means or step for performing a specified function without the recital of structure, material, or acts in support thereof, and such claim shall be construed to

[3] Graver Tank was decided over a vigorous dissent. In that dissent, Justice Black raised the first three of petitioner's four arguments against the doctrine of equivalents. See 339 U.S., at 613–614, 70 S.Ct., at 858–859 (doctrine inconsistent with statutory requirement to "distinctly claim" the invention); id., at 614–615, 70 S.Ct., at 859–860 (patent reissue process available to correct mistakes); id., at 615, n. 3, 70 S.Ct., at 859, n. 3 (duty lies with the Patent Office to examine claims and to conform them to the scope of the invention; inventors may appeal Patent Office determinations if they disagree with result).

Indeed, petitioner's first argument was not new even in 1950. Nearly 100 years before Graver Tank, this Court approved of the doctrine of equivalents in Winans v. Denmead, 15 How. 330, 14 L.Ed. 717 (1854). The dissent in Winans unsuccessfully argued that the majority result was inconsistent with the requirement in the 1836 Patent Act that the applicant "particularly 'specify and point' out what he claims as his invention," and that the patent protected nothing more. Id., 15 How. at 347 (Campbell, J., dissenting).

[4] Petitioner argues that the evolution in patent practice from "central" claiming (describing the core principles of the invention) to "peripheral" claiming (describing the outer boundaries of the invention) requires that we treat Graver Tank as an aberration and abandon the doctrine of equivalents. Brief for Petitioner 43–45. We disagree. The suggested change in claiming practice predates Graver Tank, is not of statutory origin, and seems merely to reflect narrower inventions in more crowded arts. Also, judicial recognition of so-called "pioneer" patents suggests that the abandonment of "central" claiming may be overstated. That a claim describing a limited improvement in a crowded field will have a limited range of permissible equivalents does not negate the availability of the doctrine vel non.

cover the corresponding structure, material, or acts described in the specification and *equivalents thereof*." (Emphasis added.)

Thus, under this new provision, an applicant can describe an element of his invention by the result accomplished or the function served, rather than describing the item or element to be used (e.g., "a means of connecting Part A to Part B," rather than "a two-penny nail"). Congress enacted § 112, ¶ 6 in response to Halliburton Oil Well Cementing Co. v. Walker, which rejected claims that "do not describe the invention but use 'conveniently functional language at the exact point of novelty,' "329 U.S. 1, 8, 67 S.Ct. 6, 9–10, 91 L.Ed. 3 (1946) (citation omitted). See In re Donaldson Co., 16 F.3d 1189, 1194 (C.A.Fed.1994) (Congress enacted predecessor of § 112, ¶ 6 in response to Halliburton); In re Fuetterer, 50 C.C.P.A. 1453, 319 F.2d 259, 264, n. 11 (1963) (same); see also, 2 D. Chisum, Patents § 8.04[2], at 63–64 (1996) (discussing 1954 commentary of then-Chief Patent Examiner P.J. Federico). Section 112, ¶ 6 now expressly allows so-called "means" claims, with the proviso that application of the broad literal language of such claims must be limited to only those means that are "equivalent" to the actual means shown in the patent specification. This is an application of the doctrine of equivalents in a restrictive role, narrowing the application of broad literal claim elements. We recognized this type of role for the doctrine of equivalents in Graver Tank itself. 339 U.S., at 608–609, 70 S.Ct., at 856–857. The added provision, however, is silent on the doctrine of equivalents as applied where there is no literal infringement.

Because § 112, ¶ 6 was enacted as a targeted cure to a specific problem, and because the reference in that provision to "equivalents" appears to be no more than a prophylactic against potential side effects of that cure, such limited congressional action should not be overread for negative implications. Congress in 1952 could easily have responded to Graver Tank as it did to the Halliburton decision. But it did not. Absent something more compelling than the dubious negative inference offered by petitioner, the lengthy history of the doctrine of equivalents strongly supports adherence to our refusal in Graver Tank to find that the Patent Act conflicts with that doctrine. Congress can legislate the doctrine of equivalents out of existence any time it chooses. The various policy arguments now made by both sides are thus best addressed to Congress, not this Court.

B

We do, however, share the concern of the dissenters below that the doctrine of equivalents, as it has come to be applied since Graver Tank, has taken on a life of its own, unbounded by the patent claims. There can be no denying that the doctrine of equivalents, when applied broadly, conflicts with the definitional and public-notice functions of the statutory claiming requirement. Judge Nies identified one means of avoiding this conflict:

"[A] distinction can be drawn that is not too esoteric between substitution of an equivalent for a component *in* an invention and enlarging the metes and bounds of the invention *beyond* what is claimed.

. . . . .

"Where a claim to an invention is expressed as a combination of elements, as here, 'equivalents' in the sobriquet 'Doctrine of Equivalents' refers to the equivalency of an *element* or *part* of the invention with one that is substituted in the accused product or process.

. . .

"This view that the accused device or process must be more than 'equivalent' *overall* reconciles the Supreme Court's position on infringement by equivalents with its concurrent statements that 'the courts have no right to enlarge a patent beyond the scope of its claims as allowed by the Patent Office.' [Citations omitted.] The 'scope' is not enlarged if courts do not go beyond the substitution of equivalent elements." 62 F.3d, at 1573–1574 (Nies, J., dissenting) (emphasis in original).

We concur with this apt reconciliation of our two lines of precedent. Each element contained in a patent claim is deemed material to defining the scope of the patented invention, and thus the doctrine of equivalents must be applied to individual elements of the claim, not to the invention as a whole. It is important to ensure that the application of the doctrine, even as to an individual element, is not allowed such broad play as to effectively eliminate that element in its entirety. So long as the doctrine of equivalents does not encroach beyond the limits just described, or beyond related limits to be discussed infra, at 1047–1048, 1053, n. 8, and 1054–1055, we are confident that the doctrine will not vitiate the central functions of the patent claims themselves.

III

Understandably reluctant to assume this Court would overrule Graver Tank, petitioner has offered alternative arguments in favor of a more restricted doctrine of equivalents than it feels was applied in this case. We address each in turn.

A

Petitioner first argues that Graver Tank never purported to supersede a well-established limit on non-literal infringement, known variously as "prosecution history estoppel" and "file wrapper estoppel." See Bayer Aktiengesellschaft v. Duphar Int'l Research B.V., 738 F.2d 1237, 1238 (C.A.Fed.1984). According to petitioner, any surrender of subject matter during patent prosecution, regardless of the reason for such surrender, precludes recapturing any part of that subject matter, even if it is equivalent to the matter expressly claimed. Because, during patent prosecution, respondent limited the pH element of its claim to pH levels between 6.0 and 9.0, petitioner would have those limits form bright lines beyond which no equivalents may be claimed. Any inquiry into the reasons for a surrender, petitioner claims, would undermine the public's right to clear notice of the scope of the patent as embodied in the patent file.

We can readily agree with petitioner that Graver Tank did not dispose of prosecution history estoppel as a legal limitation on the doctrine of equivalents. But petitioner reaches too far in arguing that the reason for an amendment during patent prosecution is irrelevant to any subsequent estoppel. In each of our cases cited by petitioner and by the dissent below, prosecution history estoppel was tied to amendments made to avoid the prior art, or otherwise to address a specific concern—such as obviousness—that arguably would have rendered the claimed subject matter unpatentable.

It is telling that in each case this Court probed the reasoning behind the Patent Office's insistence upon a change in the claims. In each instance, a change was demanded because the claim as otherwise written was viewed as not describing a patentable invention at all—typically because what it described was encompassed within the prior art. But, as the United States informs us, there are a variety of other reasons why the PTO may request a change in claim language. Brief for United States as Amicus Curiae 22–23 (counsel for the PTO also appearing on the brief). And if the PTO has been requesting changes in claim language without the intent to limit equivalents or, indeed, with the expectation that language it required would in many cases allow for a range of equivalents, we should be extremely reluctant to upset the basic assumptions of the PTO without substantial reason for doing so. Our prior cases have consistently applied prosecution history estoppel only where claims have been amended for a limited set of reasons, and we see no substantial cause for requiring a more rigid rule invoking an estoppel regardless of the reasons for a change.

In this case, the patent examiner objected to the patent claim due to a perceived overlap with the Booth patent, which revealed an ultrafiltration process operating at a pH above 9.0. In response to this objection, the phrase "at a pH from approximately 6.0 to 9.0" was added to the claim. While it is undisputed that the upper limit of 9.0 was added in order to distinguish the Booth patent, the reason for adding the lower limit of 6.0 is unclear. The lower limit certainly did not serve to distinguish the Booth patent, which said nothing about pH levels below 6.0. Thus, while a lower limit of 6.0, by its mere inclusion, became a material element of the claim, that did not necessarily preclude the application of the doctrine of equivalents as to that element.[5]

We are left with the problem, however, of what to do in a case like the one at bar, where the record seems not to reveal the reason for including

---

[5] We do not suggest that, where a change is made to overcome an objection based on the prior art, a court is free to review the correctness of that objection when deciding whether to apply prosecution history estoppel. As petitioner rightly notes, such concerns are properly addressed on direct appeal from the denial of a patent, and will not be revisited in an infringement action. What is permissible for a court to explore is the reason (right or wrong) for the objection and the manner in which the amendment addressed and avoided the objection.

the lower pH limit of 6.0. In our view, holding that certain reasons for a claim amendment may avoid the application of prosecution history estoppel is not tantamount to holding that the absence of a reason for an amendment may similarly avoid such an estoppel. Mindful that claims do indeed serve both a definitional and a notice function, we think the better rule is to place the burden on the patent-holder to establish the reason for an amendment required during patent prosecution. The court then would decide whether that reason is sufficient to overcome prosecution history estoppel as a bar to application of the doctrine of equivalents to the element added by that amendment. Where no explanation is established, however, the court should presume that the PTO had a substantial reason related to patentability for including the limiting element added by amendment. In those circumstances, prosecution history estoppel would bar the application of the doctrine equivalents as to that element. The presumption we have described, one subject to rebuttal if an appropriate reason for a required amendment is established, gives proper deference to the role of claims in defining an invention and providing public notice, and to the primacy of the PTO in ensuring that the claims allowed cover only subject matter that is properly patentable in a proffered patent application. Applied in this fashion, prosecution history estoppel places reasonable limits on the doctrine of equivalents, and further insulates the doctrine from any feared conflict with the Patent Act.

Because respondent has not proffered in this Court a reason for the addition of a lower pH limit, it is impossible to tell whether the reason for that addition could properly avoid an estoppel. Whether a reason in fact exists, but simply was not adequately developed, we cannot say. On remand, the Federal Circuit can consider whether reasons for that portion of the amendment were offered or not and whether further opportunity to establish such reasons would be proper.

B

Petitioner next argues that even if Graver Tank remains good law, the case held only that the absence of substantial differences was a necessary element for infringement under the doctrine of equivalents, not that it was sufficient for such a result. Brief for Petitioner 32. Relying on Graver Tank's references to the problem of an "unscrupulous copyist" and "piracy," 339 U.S., at 607, 70 S.Ct., at 855–856, petitioner would require judicial exploration of the equities of a case before allowing application of the doctrine of equivalents. To be sure, Graver Tank refers to the prevention of copying and piracy when describing the benefits of the doctrine of equivalents. That the doctrine produces such benefits, however, does not mean that its application is limited only to cases where those particular benefits are obtained.

Elsewhere in Graver Tank the doctrine is described in more neutral terms. And the history of the doctrine as relied upon by Graver Tank reflects a basis for the doctrine not so limited as petitioner would have it. In Winans v. Denmead, 15 How. 330, 343, 14 L.Ed. 717 (1854), we described the doctrine of equivalents as growing out of a legally implied term in each patent claim that "the claim extends to the thing patented, however its form or proportions may be varied." Under that view, application of the doctrine of equivalents involves determining whether a particular accused product or process infringes upon the patent claim, where the claim takes the form—half express, half implied—of "X and its equivalents."

Union Paper–Bag Machine Co. v. Murphy, 97 U.S. 120, 125, 24 L.Ed. 935 (1878), on which Graver Tank also relied, offers a similarly intent-neutral view of the doctrine of equivalents:

> "[T]he substantial equivalent of a thing, in the sense of the patent law, is the same as the thing itself; so that if two devices do the same work in substantially the same way, and accomplish substantially the same result, they are the same, even though they differ in name, form, or shape."

If the essential predicate of the doctrine of equivalents is the notion of identity between a patented invention and its equivalent, there is no basis for treating an infringing equivalent any differently than a device that infringes the express terms of the patent. Application of the doctrine of equivalents, therefore, is akin to determining literal infringement, and neither requires proof of intent.

Petitioner also points to Graver Tank's seeming reliance on the absence of independent experimentation by the alleged infringer as supporting an equitable defense to the doctrine of equivalents. The Federal Circuit explained this factor by suggesting that an alleged infringer's behavior, be it copying, designing around a patent, or independent experimentation, indirectly reflects the substantiality of the differences between the patented invention and the accused device or process. According to the Federal Circuit, a person aiming to copy or aiming to avoid a patent is imagined to be at least marginally skilled at copying or avoidance, and thus intentional copying raises an inference—rebuttable by proof of independent development—of having only insubstantial differences, and intentionally designing around a patent claim raises an inference of substantial differences. This explanation leaves much to be desired. At a minimum, one wonders how ever to distinguish between the intentional copyist making minor changes to lower the risk of legal action, and the incremental innovator designing around the claims, yet seeking to capture as much as is permissible of the patented advance.

But another explanation is available that does not require a divergence from generally objective principles of patent infringement. In both instances in Graver Tank where we referred to independent research or experiments, we were discussing the known interchangeability between the chemical compound claimed in the patent and the compound substituted by the alleged infringer. The need for independent experimentation thus could reflect knowledge—or lack thereof—of interchangeability possessed by one presumably skilled in the art. The known interchangeability of substitutes for an element of a patent is one of the express objective factors noted by Graver Tank as bearing upon whether the accused device is substantially the same as the patented invention. Independent experimentation by the alleged infringer would not always reflect upon the objective question whether a person skilled in the art would have known of the interchangeability between two elements, but in many cases it would likely be probative of such knowledge.

Although Graver Tank certainly leaves room for petitioner's suggested inclusion of intent-based elements in the doctrine of equivalents, we do not read it as requiring them. The better view, and the one consistent with Graver Tank's predecessors and the objective approach to infringement, is that intent plays no role in the application of the doctrine of equivalents.

C

Finally, petitioner proposes that in order to minimize conflict with the notice function of patent claims, the doctrine of equivalents should be limited to equivalents that are disclosed within the patent itself. A milder version of this argument, which found favor with the dissenters below, is that the doctrine should be limited to equivalents that were known at the time the patent was issued, and should not extend to after-arising equivalents.

As we have noted, supra, at 1052, with regard to the objective nature of the doctrine, a skilled practitioner's knowledge of the interchangeability between claimed and accused elements is not relevant for its own sake, but rather for what it tells the fact-finder about the similarities or differences between those elements. Much as the perspective of the hypothetical "reasonable person" gives content to concepts such as "negligent" behavior, the perspective of a skilled practitioner provides content to, and limits on, the concept of "equivalence." Insofar as the question under the doctrine of equivalents is whether an accused element is equivalent to a claimed element, the proper time for evaluating equivalency—and thus knowledge of interchangeability between elements—is at the time of infringement, not at the time the patent was issued. And rejecting the milder version of petitioner's argument necessarily rejects the more severe proposition that equivalents must not only be known, but must also be actually disclosed in the patent in order for such equivalents to infringe upon the patent.

IV

[In this part, the Court defers to another day the issue of whether equivalence should be determined by the court or by the jury. Thus, it left standing the Federal Circuit's decision to allow a jury to apply the doctrine of equivalents.]

V

All that remains is to address the debate regarding the linguistic framework under which "equivalence" is determined. Both the parties and the Federal Circuit spend considerable time arguing whether the so-called "triple identity" test—focusing on the function served by a particular claim element, the way that element serves that function, and the result thus obtained by that element—is a suitable method for determining equivalence, or whether an "insubstantial differences" approach is better. There seems to be substantial agreement that, while the triple identity test may be suitable for analyzing mechanical devices, it often provides a poor framework for analyzing other products or processes. On the other hand, the insubstantial differences test offers little additional guidance as to what might render any given difference "insubstantial."

In our view, the particular linguistic framework used is less important than whether the test is probative of the essential inquiry: Does the accused product or process contain elements identical or equivalent to each claimed element of the patented invention? Different linguistic frameworks may be more suitable to different cases, depending on their particular facts. A focus on individual elements and a special vigilance against allowing the concept of equivalence to eliminate completely any such elements should reduce considerably the imprecision of whatever language is used. An analysis of the role played by each element in the context of the specific patent claim will thus inform the inquiry as to whether a substitute element matches the function, way, and result of the claimed element, or whether the substitute element plays a role substantially different from the claimed element. With these limiting principles as a backdrop, we see no purpose in going further and micro-managing the Federal Circuit's particular word-choice for analyzing equivalence. We expect that the Federal Circuit will refine the formulation of the test for equivalence in the orderly course of case-by-case determinations, and we leave such refinement to that court's sound judgment in this area of its special expertise.

VI

Today we adhere to the doctrine of equivalents. The determination of equivalence should be applied as an objective inquiry on an element-by-element basis. Prosecution history estoppel continues to be available as a defense to infringement, but if the patent-holder demonstrates that an amendment required during prosecution had a purpose unrelated to patentability, a court must consider that purpose in order to decide whether an estoppel is precluded. Where the patentholder is unable to establish such a purpose, a court should presume that the purpose behind the required amendment is such that prosecution history estoppel would apply. Because the Court of Appeals for the Federal Circuit did not consider all of the requirements as described by us today, particularly as related to prosecution history estoppel and the preservation of some meaning for each element in a claim, we reverse and remand for further proceedings consistent with this opinion.

It is so ordered.

JUSTICE GINSBURG, with whom JUSTICE KENNEDY joins, concurring.

I join the opinion of the Court and write separately to add a cautionary note on the rebuttable presumption the Court announces regarding prosecution history estoppel. I address in particular the application of the presumption in this case and others in which patent prosecution has already been completed. The new presumption, if applied woodenly, might in some instances unfairly discount the expectations of a patentee who had no notice at the time of patent prosecution that such a presumption would apply. Such a patentee would have had little incentive to insist that the reasons for all modifications be memorialized in the file wrapper as they were made. Years after the fact, the patentee may find it difficult to establish an evidentiary basis that would overcome the new presumption. The Court's opinion is sensitive to this problem, noting that "the PTO may have relied upon a flexible rule of estoppel when deciding whether to ask for a change" during patent prosecution. Ante, at 1050, n. 6.

Because respondent has not presented to this Court any explanation for the addition of the lower pH limit, I concur in the decision to remand the matter to the Federal Circuit. On remand, that court can determine—bearing in mind the prior absence of clear rules of the game—whether suitable reasons for including the lower pH limit were earlier offered or, if not, whether they can now be established.

Insert in lieu of *Aro Manufacturing* on page 749, or in addition to *Aro* on page 753:

Sandvik Aktiebolag v. E.J. Co.

United States Court of Appeals for the Federal Circuit, 1997.
121 F.3d 669.

■ ARACHER, CHIEF JUDGE.

Sandvik Aktiebolag (Sandvik) appeals the order of the United States District Court for the Middle District of Tennessee, No. 3–94–1076, granting summary judgment of noninfringement in favor of defendant E.J. Company (E.J.). The district court held that United States Patent No. 4,222,690 (the '690 patent) and United States Patent No. 4,381,162 (the '162 patent) were not infringed because defendant's replacement of the carbide tip of the drill constituted a permissible repair. We reverse.

BACKGROUND

The facts in this case are not in dispute. The patents in suit are directed to a drill with a shank portion and a unique carbide tip geometry that has specially configured cutting edges resulting in a drill suitable for high-feed machining with improved cutting ability especially at its center portion. The drill tip is not separately patented. The drill shank is made of medium carbon steel. The drill tip is made of a more durable carbide and is brazed to the steel shank. Brazing is like soldering but with a much higher melting point. It requires a temperature of 1300 degrees Fahrenheit to join the carbide tip to the steel shank.

Sandvik manufactures a commercial embodiment of the patented drill. Although made of durable carbide, over time and use, the drill tip dulls and may require resharpening. Resharpening, also known as regrinding, involves putting a new edge on the drill tip. Normally, the drill can cut through about one thousand inches of material before needing resharpening, depending, of course, upon the hardness of the material being cut. Sandvik expects the drill tip to be resharpened and, in fact, issues guidelines explaining how to resharpen the tip so as to maintain the specially configured cutting edges. Sandvik does not contend that resharpening constitutes infringement.

E.J. offers a drill repair service which includes resharpening and retipping Sandvik drills. E.J. retips, at the request of its customers, when the tip cannot be sharpened because it chips, cracks or simply wears down after being resharpened several times. According to E.J's vice-president, Mr. Robert Hayes, some of E.J.'s customers elect not to have the drill retipped when it cannot be resharpened any longer. E.J. returns the drill to the customer or disposes of it at the customer's request. The parties agree that when the tip is damaged (i.e. chipped, cracked or sufficiently worn down so that it cannot be resharpened), the drill has reached the end of its useful life unless it is retipped.

E.J.'s retipping process includes removing the worn or damaged tip by heating the tip to 1300 degrees Fahrenheit using an acetylene torch. E.J. then brazes in a rectangular piece of new carbide onto the drill shank. After the piece of carbide has cooled, E.J. recreates the patented geometry of the cutting edges by machining the carbide. This process includes: (1) grinding the carbide to the proper outside diameter; (2) grinding the carbide to a point; (3) grinding the rake surfaces of the new point; (4) grinding the center of the new point; and (5) honing the edges. In the final steps of the machining process, E.J. creates the cutting edges by following Sandvik's instructions for tip resharpening.

Sandvik claims that E.J.'s retipping service constitutes an infringing reconstruction of its patented drills. Sandvik does not manufacture or sell replacement drill tips. It contends that it never intended for the drills to be retipped. E.J. contends that its retipping service is a lawful repair of the patented drills.

On December 7, 1994, Sandvik filed a patent infringement suit in the United States District Court for the Middle District of Tennessee claiming that E.J.'s retipping service was an impermissible reconstruction of the patented drill and that E.J.'s actions, therefore, constituted an infringement of the '690 and '162 patents. On summary judgment, the district court held that E.J.'s retipping was a permissible repair, not a reconstruction of the drills.

DISCUSSION

                                        . . .

II.

Direct infringement includes the making of a patented article without authority. 35 U.S.C. § 271(a) (1994). Sandvik contends that E.J. is reconstructing its patented drill and therefore infringing its '690 and '162 patents under § 271(a). However, when Sandvik sold its patented drills to its customers, it granted them an implied license to use the drill for its useful life, see Aro Mfg. Co. v. Convertible Top Replacement Co., 377 U.S. 476, 484, 84 S.Ct. 1526, 1531, 12 L.Ed.2d 457 (1964) ("Aro II "), and the implied license to use includes the right to repair the patented drill, see, e.g., Standard Havens Prods., Inc. v. Gencor Indus., Inc., 953 F.2d 1360, 1376, 21 USPQ2d 1321, 1333 (Fed.Cir.1991).

The Supreme Court has taken an expansive view of what constitutes a permissible repair. In Aro Mfg. Co. v. Convertible Top Replacement Co., 365 U.S. 336, 81 S.Ct. 599, 5 L.Ed.2d 592 (1961) ("Aro I "), the Court held that the replacement of the fabric portion of a convertible car top was a permissible repair, not an infringing reconstruction. 365 U.S. at 346, 81 S.Ct. at 604–05. The Court held: "No element, not itself separately patented, that constitutes one of the elements of a combination patent is entitled to patent monopoly, however essential it may be to the patented combination and no matter how costly or difficult replacement may be." Id. at 345, 81 S.Ct. at 604. Therefore, even if E.J.'s retipping service cost almost as much as the drill or if the replacement of the tip is difficult and time consuming, as in this case, these factors are not dispositive of reconstruction.

The Court also rejected the "heart of the invention test." See id. at 344–45, 81 S.Ct. at 603–04 (holding that replacement of the distinguishing part of the patented combination does not amount to a reconstruction because a patent covers the totality of the elements in a combination); see also Dawson Chem. Co. v. Rohm & Haas Co., 448 U.S. 176, 217 (This Court has "eschewed the suggestion that the legal distinction between 'reconstruction' and 'repair' should be affected by whether the element of the combination that has been replaced is an 'essential' or 'distinguishing' part of the invention.") (citing Aro I, 365 U.S. at 344, 81 S.Ct. at 603–04); Sage Prods. Inc. v. Devon Indus., Inc., 45 F.3d at 1575, 1577, 33 USPQ2d 1765,

1767 ("The size or relative importance of the replacement part to the patented combination is not relevant when determining whether conduct constitutes repair or replacement."). Therefore, the fact that E.J. may be replacing the novel features of the '690 patented invention is also not dispositive of reconstruction.

In Aro I, the Supreme Court further explained the test for what constitutes a reconstruction: "The decisions of this Court require the conclusion that reconstruction of a patented entity, comprised of unpatented elements, is limited to such a true reconstruction of the entity as to 'in fact make a new article,' after the entity, viewed as a whole, has become spent." 365 U.S. at 346, 81 S.Ct. at 604 (citations omitted). Although we question the district court's finding that the tip is, in fact, a separate part of the device, we need not reach this issue because the court nevertheless failed to analyze whether the replacement of this "part" constituted reconstruction consistent with Aro I.

There are a number of factors to consider in determining whether a defendant has made a new article, after the device has become spent, including the nature of the actions by the defendant, the nature of the device and how it is designed (namely, whether one of the components of the patented combination has a shorter useful life than the whole), whether a market has developed to manufacture or service the part at issue and objective evidence of the intent of the patentee. Under the totality of the circumstances, we hold in this case that E.J.'s actions are a reconstruction.

By E.J.'s own admission, the drill is "spent" when the tip can no longer be resharpened unless it is retipped. In fact, the record reveals that E.J.'s customers may elect not to retip and inform E.J. to discard the drill instead.

Moreover, the nature of the work done by E.J. shows that retipping is more like reconstruction than repair. E.J. does not just attach a new part for a worn part, but rather must go though several steps to replace, configure and integrate the tip onto the shank. It has to break the worn or damaged tip from the shank by heating it to 1300 degrees Fahrenheit. It brazes to the shank a new rectangular block of carbide and grinds and machines it to the proper diameter and creates the point. Thereafter, the tip is honed and sharpened, grinding the rake surfaces and the center of the point and honing the edges. These actions are effectively a re-creation of the patented invention after it is spent.

This is not a case where it is clear that the patented device has a useful life much longer than that of certain parts which wear out quickly. For example, in Wilson v. Simpson, 50 U.S. (9 How.) 109, 125–26, 13 L.Ed. 66 (1850), in determining that a repair had occurred, the Supreme Court focused specifically on the fact that the machine was designed so that the knives had to be replaced long before the other components:

> The proof in the case, is, that one of [the patentee's] machines, properly made, will last in use for several years, but that its cutting-knives will wear out and must be replaced at least every sixty or ninety days.

> . . .

> [If such a] part of the combination is meant to be only temporary in the use of the whole, and to be frequently replaced, because it will not last as long as the other parts of the combination, its inventor cannot complain.

50 U.S. (9 How.) at 125–26, 13 L.Ed. 66. See also Aro I, 365 U.S. at 337–38, 81 S.Ct. at 600 (noting that the fabric had a much shorter expected life (about three years) than the convertible car top); Porter v. Farmer Supply Serv., Inc., 790 F.2d 882, 883, 229 USPQ 814, 814 (Fed.Cir.1986) ("The useful life of a disk is measured in weeks, that of a harvester is five or six years. The district court found, and it is undisputed, that a purchaser can expect to wear out many disks during the useful life of the header.").

The drill tip in this case is not a part like the detachable knives in the Wilson that have to be replaced periodically over the useful life of the planing machine. The drill tip was not manufactured to be a replaceable part, although it could be resharpened a number of times to extend its life. It was not intended or expected to have a life of temporary duration in comparison to the drill shank. And finally, the tip was not attached to the shank in a manner to be easily detachable.

In Aro I, the Supreme Court also noted that "the consequent demand for replacement fabrics has given rise to a substantial industry." Evidence of development in the industry could also be a factor tending to prove that there is a reasonable expectation that the part of the patented combination wears out quickly and requires frequent replacement. See also Kendall Co. v. Progressive Medical Tech., Inc., 85 F.3d 1570, 1572, 38 USPQ2d 1917, 1919 (Fed.Cir.1996) ("The resulting market for replacement sleeves has been substantial."); Sage Prods., 45 F.3d at 1577, 33 USPQ2d at 1766 (noting that "[t]he sale of replacement inner containers is a sizable market."). In this case, there is no evidence of a substantial market for drill retipping of the sort required for the Sandvik drill. There is no evidence of large numbers of customers retipping these drills or of companies (other than E.J.) offering to retip these drills. No one manufactures replacement tips for Sandvik's drill and although some customers opt to retip the drill only a small percentage of all drills manufactured are retipped.

Finally, there was no intent evidenced by the patentee that would support E.J.'s argument that replacement of the tips is a repair. See Kendall Co., 85 F.3d at 1575, 38 USPQ2d at 1921 (replacing the sleeve in a medical device which applies pressure to patients' limbs was a repair noting that the manufacturer "clearly intended to permit its customers to replace the sleeves" and actually sold replacement sleeves); Sage Prods., 45 F.3d at 1578–79, 33 USPQ2d at 1767–68 (evidence that patentee intended the inner containers to be replaced, that it manufactures replacement parts and instructs customers to replace supports holding such replacement a

permissible repair); Porter, 790 F.2d at 885–86, 229 USPQ at 816–17 (considering that the patentee sold replacement cutting disks for its tomato harvester). The evidence shows that Sandvik never intended for its drills to be retipped. It did not manufacture or sell replacement drill tips. It did not publish instructions on how to retip its patented drills or suggest that the drills could or should be retipped. Sandvik was aware that the drill tip would need occasional resharpening and instructed its customer on how to resharpen the tip. There is, therefore, no objective evidence that Sandvik's drill tip was intended to be a replaceable part. Although the repair or reconstruction issue does not turn on the intention of the patentee alone, the fact that no replacement drill tips have ever been made or sold by the patentee is consistent with the conclusion that replacement of the carbide tip is not a permissible repair.

Although there is no bright-line test for determining whether reconstruction or repair has occurred, we conclude based on all of the facts in this case that E.J. is reconstructing an otherwise spent device when it retips Sandvik's drills. Accordingly, we hold that E.J.'s drill tip replacements infringe the '690 and '162 patents. Because there are no disputed issues of fact, we reverse the district court grant of summary judgment.

NOTES

Insert at page 757, in lieu of Note 2:

2. *Infringement under the doctrine of equivalents.* Given the care with which patent applications are drafted and examined, is there any justification for allowing patentees to argue that devices or processes that are not within the literal ambit of their patents nonetheless infringe? One explanation is that the doctrine of equivalents mirrors the policies of copyright and trademark law. A cause of action to prevent express infringement is thought not sufficient protection for the right holder because it would be too easy to make a trivial variation and capture a part of the market. Thus, some leeway is created by permitting the patentee to show that the defendant has an obvious variation on the patented invention.

Some commentators, however, offer a different explanation for this doctrine. Looking back at older case law, they explain the doctrine as concerned with mistakes—that is, as allowing the patentee to stretch the claims to cover things he should have claimed, but inadvertently omitted. These commentators argue that the patent reward is an important part of the system for encouraging innovation. Inventive activities would be chilled if inventors knew that simple errors might bar them from receiving their expected returns.

A related justification for the doctrine of equivalents can be called the "quasi-mistake" approach. It recognizes the dynamic quality of innovation. Under this view, patentees cannot be expected to claim every variation on their invention because some variations only become possible because of developments in other fields. *Hughes* is an example: the developments in the computer field that made an onboard processor possible mostly occurred after the *Hughes* patent issued. If the patentee is to capture the rewards of inventing, the variations made possible through later developments ought to be considered infringing.

Do any of these explanations make sense? The defect in the copyright/trademark analogy is that the extensive patent application process gives the patent holder ample opportunity to identify the exact inventive concept and claim all the obvious changes that could be made in it. Thus, there is little need to give the patentee extra leeway at the infringement stage. As to the mistake ideas: is not a mistake the worst case for the doctrine? After all, the burden of error must fall somewhere; putting it on the patentee encourages accurate claiming.

Besides, and as *Warner-Jenkinson* notes, the 1952 Act has its own solution for these problems. As to leeway, the last paragraph of § 112 allows the patentee to claim inventions of more than one element ("combinations") by expressing "a means ... for performing a specified function." An illustration of this "means plus function" claiming can be found in the Lipschitz patent of Assignment 15. It allows the patentee to extend the reach of her patent to *literally* cover other embodiments of the inventive concept, including some that could not have been foreseen at the time the claims were drafted. For mistake, the reissue provisions of §§ 251–252 give patentees a two-year window in which to correct for error. This provision has an important advantage over common law, for it also protects the public. It gives those who practiced the invention in reliance on the original patent "intervening rights," meaning the right to continue any activity that began before the reissue. Does Justice Thomas offer a convincing explanation for retaining the doctrine after the 1952 Act? As Note 4 describes, the doctrine has generated considerable difficulties—which is precisely why the Supreme Court chose to reexamine it in *Warner-Jenkinson.*

Insert at page 759, in lieu of Note 4:

4. *Brakes on the doctrine of equivalents.* Should the process used by Warner–Jenkinson be deemed to infringe Hilton Davis's patent? The pH of the Warner–Jenkinson method is only 1 unit below the pH level claimed (5 as opposed to 6). However, as the court notes in its first footnote, pH—which quantifies the concentration of hydrogen ions in solution—is measured on a logarithmic scale. Thus, Warner–Jenkinson's filtration method runs in a solution that has 10 times more hydrogen ions than Hilton–Davis's method; the average chemist might consider this a significant difference even if it does seem like much to the average lawyer.

Indeed, many devices perform the same function in the same way to achieve the same result. *Graver Tank*'s "triple identity" (or tripartite) function/way/result test has, in fact, been very controversial. If applied literally, it would stifle inventiveness for the reasons set out in Note 3.

Moreover, as the pH problem demonstrates, unchecked use of the doctrine can make it difficult for third parties (such as chemists) to know when their activity will be deemed to infringe. *Warner-Jenkinson* reached the Supreme Court after considerable efforts by the CAFC to limit the reach of the doctrine. Consider the limitations that the CAFC has, in the past, proposed: which are now ruled out by the Supreme Court's opinion? Which were adopted? Do you agree with the Supreme Court's choices?

a. *Nonobviousness.* One of the oldest limits on the doctrine of equivalents is that the patentee cannot use it to stretch the patent to encompass activity that would have been considered obvious (or non-novel) at the time he made his invention. That is, the doctrine cannot be used to acquire exclusive rights over inventions that could not have been patented in the first place. In *Wilson Sporting Goods Co. v. David Geoffrey & Assoc.,*[6] Judge Rich attempted to make this analysis easier. He suggested constructing a hypothetical claim that would cover the accused product. Then, ask whether that claim could have been patented at the time the application on the patent in issue was pending.

b. *Prosecution history estoppel.* Note 1(a) described use of prosecution history estoppel to prevent patentees from interpreting claims in a manner that would resurrect rights to inventions that were expressly relinquished. It is used in a similar way when the doctrine of equivalents is raised, for the patentee is also precluded from using this doctrine to capture technology that was described in claims that were relinquished during prosecution to avoid prior art. Do you agree with the majority or concurrence as to who should bear the burden of showing why relinquishment occurred?

So far, there has been very little explication of how patentees can meet this burden, especially with respect to patents that were allowed before it became clear how important the reason for relinquishment would be. *Warner-Jenkinson* has also spawned confusion on the question of what "a purpose unrelated to patentability" means. Since every amendment—even one directed at nothing more than making a drawing easier to read—has some relation to patentability, a literal reading of the opinion would make prosecution history estoppel unavailable to every patentee who made any amendment. That would certainly chill the willingness of applicants to agree with examiners! The Federal Circuit has taken a more modest approach, one in line with prior practice. For example, in Bai v. L & L Wings, Inc.,[7] the court stated: "The meaning of the word 'patentability' was not made clear [by the *Warner-Jenkinson* Court], but the context of the court's discussion was patentability over the prior art."

c. *The every-element test.* Lately, the CAFC has stressed the fact that the every-element test applies as much to infringement under the doctrine of equivalents as it does to literal infringement. In *Pennwalt Corp. v.*

---

[6] 904 F.2d 677 (Fed.Cir.1990).   [7] 32160 F.3d 1350, 1355 (Fed. Cir. 1998).

Durand–Wayland, Inc.,[8] for example, the court required that the accused device contain an equivalent to each and every element of the patented invention. In that case, both inventions sorted fruit by color and weight. The patented invention had discrete electrical components and the progress of the fruit through the sorter could be continuously observed on monitoring equipment. The accused device was computerized. Although it might have been possible to program the equipment to monitor the fruit's progress, it was not so programmed. The court held that there was no infringement under the doctrine of equivalents because the accused device did not have an equivalent to the patented invention's progress tracker.

The courts following *Pennwalt* did not find the "all-elements" test, as the CAFC calls it, easy to apply. Since the Patent Act does not require patentees to separately identify the elements of their claims, there can be considerable uncertainty as to what features of the patented invention must be duplicated by the accused device. Further, the differences between the accused invention and the patented invention that make literal infringement unavailable, also tend to obscure the element by element comparison.[9]

d. *Insubstantiality*. In the lower court opinion in *Warner-Jenkinson*, the majority held that "the doctrine [of equivalents] applies if, and only if, the differences between the claimed and accused products or processes are insubstantial." Thus, even if an invention meets the function/way/result test, it will not be considered to infringe if it represents a substantially different product or process from the patented one. The court indicated that the factors to be considered in determining insubstantiality include: 1) whether persons with skill in the art actually knew of the equivalence of the claimed and accused inventions, 2) whether a person with skill could have known of the equivalence, and 3) whether the defendant had intended to copy (which could imply that it was only interested in making trivial changes), or had intended to design around (which could imply that it had attempted to make significant changes), or had inadvertently arrived at the same invention through independent research.[10]

e. *Copying*. Some of the dissenters to the CAFC's opinion in *Warner-Jenkinson* would have looked more closely at the behavior of the alleged infringer. Judge Lourie, for example, would have made only those who proceeded in bad faith to free ride on the patentee (i.e. copyists) vulnerable to infringement under the doctrine. Those who independently invent or who were seeking to "invent around" the patent would not have been

---

[8] 833 F.2d 931 (Fed.Cir.1987), cert. denied, 485 U.S. 961, 108 S.Ct. 1226, 99 L.Ed.2d 426 (1988).

[9] See, e.g., Corning Glass Works v. Sumitomo Electric U.S.A., Inc., 868 F.2d 1251 (Fed.Cir.1989).

[10] Hilton Davis Chemical Co. v. Warner—Jenkinson Co., 62 F.3d 1512 (Fed.Cir. 1995)(en banc).

liable for infringement even if they came rather close to the patented invention.

f. *Obfuscation.* Judge Lourie would also have considered the behavior of the patentee. Because notice is an important function of the claiming provisions, he would have denied resort to the doctrine of equivalents to patentees who "impair the ability of the public to reasonably understand from the claims what is patented" and also to those who failed to seek reissue when it was available.

Insert at page 760, in lieu of Note 5:

5. *The role of the jury.* Until fairly recently, most patent disputes were tried to the trial judge. However, that practice began to change in the mid-1980's, when increasingly, parties began to exercise their Seventh Amendment rights to trials by jury. It is not clear why this change has occurred. Some commentators attribute it to the establishment of the court of appeals for the federal circuit. Because the standard for setting aside jury verdicts is somewhat more rigorous than the standard for setting aside judicial findings, it is possible that some attorneys have been using juries to insulate their trial-court "wins" from scrutiny by the patent experts who sit on the CAFC. Another explanation is that patentees have discovered that juries tend to favor inventors over infringers, especially in the situation where the inventor is an american (or an individual) and the infringer is a foreigner (or a corporation).

No matter what the explanation, this change in practice has been a major concern to both the Supreme Court and the CAFC. Jury trials are more expensive and slower than bench trials. They also use up more judicial resources. In addition, there is a concern that jurors may be less able to cope with the technical issues raised by patent cases, leading to more incorrect and more unpredictable decisionmaking. In Markman v. Westview Instruments, Inc.,[11] the Supreme Court acknowledged some of these concerns, holding that even in jury tried cases, the issue of claim interpretation—that is, the issue in *Fromson*—is to be decided by the judge. The Court reasoned that claim construction is neither clearly a question of law (which is always tried to the court) nor clearly a question of fact (which, under the Seventh Amendment, is within the province of the jury in actions at law). Accordingly, "functional considerations" should apply to determine the applicability of the Seventh Amendment. Since judges are better than juries at construing written instruments, the Court found that it makes sense to give judges the duty to interpret patent claims. That allocation of authority has the added benefit of allowing stare decisis to control claim interpretation, with the result that the same claim will always be interpreted in the same way, thereby making for a more stable and predictable patent system.

[11] 517 U.S. 370, 116 S.Ct. 1384, 134 L.Ed.2d 577 (1996).

Warner-Jenkinson also involved a question of allocating decisional authority, this time with respect to the application of the doctrine of equivalents. In jury-tried cases, this issue had been submitted to the jury. After *Markman*, however, it was forcefully argued that the doctrine of equivalents could be cabined by leaving the issue to the trial judge, who is in a better position than a jury to recognize the problems created when patentees extend the scope of their claims too broadly. To deal with the Seventh Amendment guarantee of trial by jury, those favoring this allocation argued that the doctrine of equivalents was equitable in nature. Since the Seventh Amendment applies only to cases at law, it would not be unconstitutional to withdraw doctrine of equivalents issues from juries.

When *Warner-Jenkinson* was argued in the Federal Circuit, the CAFC rejected this approach, leaving the application of the doctrine of equivalents to juries.[12] The Supreme Court declined to review this part of the CAFC's decision. In an omitted part of the opinion, Justice Thomas acknowledged that giving claim interpretation to the court while leaving the doctrine of equivalents to juries would "seem at cross-purposes," but he noted that there was ample support for the CAFC's decision in prior case law. In a footnote, however, the Court did consider how jury verdicts should be scrutinized in order to impose some limits on the doctrine of equivalents:

"With regard to the concern over unreviewability due to black-box jury verdicts, we offer only guidance, not a specific mandate. Where the evidence is such that no reasonable jury could determine two elements to be equivalent, district courts are obliged to grant partial or complete summary judgment. See Fed. Rule Civ. Proc. 56; Celotex Corp. v. Catrett, 477 U.S. 317, 322–323, 106 S.Ct. 2548, 2552–2553, 91 L.Ed.2d 265 (1986). If there has been a reluctance to do so by some courts due to unfamiliarity with the subject matter, we are confident that the Federal Circuit can remedy the problem. Of course, the various legal limitations on the application of the doctrine of equivalents are to be determined by the court, either on a pretrial motion for partial summary judgment or on a motion for judgment as a matter of law at the close of the evidence and after the jury verdict. Fed. Rule Civ. Proc. 56; Fed. Rule Civ. Proc. 50. Thus, under the particular facts of a case, if prosecution history estoppel would apply or if a theory of equivalence would entirely vitiate a particular claim element, partial or complete judgment should be rendered by the court, as there would be no further material issue for the jury to resolve. Finally, in cases that reach the jury, a special verdict and/or interrogatories on each claim element could be very useful in facilitating review, uniformity, and possibly postverdict judgments as a matter of law. See Fed. Rule Civ. Proc. 49; Fed. Rule Civ. Proc. 50. We leave it to the Federal Circuit

[12] Hilton Davis Chemical Co. v. Warner—Jenkinson Co., 62 F.3d 1512, 1527–28   (Fed.Cir.1995)(en banc).

how best to implement procedural improvements to promote certainty, consistency, and reviewability to this area of the law."[13]

The upshot of *Markman* and *Warner-Jenkinson* is that there has been considerable revision in the way that patent trials are conducted. In particular, pretrial hearings have proliferated, with counsel often pushing the court to construe the claims and demark the limits of equivalence before they must choose a strategy for the jury-tried part of the case (such as the trial on infringement).

If the trial court does construe the claims pretrial, in what is now called a *"Markman* hearing," should the CAFC consider an appeal of its construction on an interlocutory basis? If the CAFC waits until final judgment, and it turns out that the claims were interpreted incorrectly, then the jury part of the case may need to be repeated. For example, in the infringement part of the case, the jury will not have been comparing the accused device to the correct claims. An immediate appeal would, however, be counter the usual federal practice of waiting until final judgment has been entered, see 28 U.S.C. § 1291. So far, the CAFC has not been willing to hear appeals on claim construction on an interlocutory basis.

Insert at page 763, after Note 10:

10. *Infringement revisited.* Is *Hughes Aircraft* correctly decided? Although the infringement issue was decided by the CAFC in 1983, the United States has managed, through a series of appeals on a variety of other issues, to keep the case alive. The Supreme Court has recently vacated judgment and remanded it to the CAFC for reconsideration in light of *Warner–Jenkinson*.[14] Over a dissent by Judges Clevenger and Gajarsa, the court refused to bite.[15]

[13] *Warner-Jenkinson*, 117 S.Ct. at 1053 n.8.

[14] United States v. Hughes Aircraft, Co., 137 U.S. 680, 117 S.Ct. 1466, 137 L.Ed.2d 680 (1997).

[15] Hughes Aircraft Co. v. U.S., 148 F.3d 1384 (Fed. Cir. 1998).

ASSIGNMENT 23

THE INTEREST IN PUBLIC ACCESS

Insert at page 783 after Note 4:

5. *Section 271(e)(1).* As noted in the casebook, after *Bolar* Congress amended § 271 to create an exemption for clinical research activities conducted "solely for uses reasonably related to the development and submission of information" to the FDA. Since its enactment, the provision has given rise to a series of district court cases on the meaning of "solely"—that is, on the scope of this defense to infringement. Some courts have read § 271(e)(1) narrowly, so that a defendant who uses its tests for any purpose other than preparing a submission to the FDA will be found to have infringed the patent.[1]

In Amgen, Inc. v. Hoechst Marion Roussel, Inc.,[2] however, a district court announced a broader scope. It held that so long as the defendant, at the time of its use, was making, using, or selling the patented invention "in ways that objectively bear reasonable prospects of yielding information that might be relevant in the FDA approval process" then subsequent use of the information for other purposes would not lead to a loss of the defense.

In the *Amgen* case, the defendant had engaged in what the plaintiff characterized as a "world-wide coordinated effort" to market the drug and to evaluate its own patent position, and was piggybacking its global efforts on the uses it made for purposes of acquiring FDA approval. Thus, the defendant exported product to Japan for use as a reference in developing a manufacturing process, tested production batches for consistency, characterized the structure of the product, exported product to Scotland to be tested for viruses and developed plans to conduct tests to comply with Japanese regulatory requirements. It had also tested the product for purity with procedures that were not later submitted to the FDA. The court held that § 271(e)(1) applied nonetheless. Planning to meet Japanese regulatory requirements is not an infringing act. All of the other activities could also be used to satisfy FDA requirements, or were attempts to develop data to satisfy the FDA and came within the scope of the exemption.

---

[1] See, e.g, Biogen, Inc. v. Schering AG, 954 F. Supp. 391 (D. Mass. 1996); Scripps Clinic & Research Found. v. Genentech, Inc., 666 F. Supp. 1379 (N.D. Cal. 1987).

[2] 46 U.S.P.Q.2d 1906, 1998 WL 195994 (D. Mass. 1998).

ASSIGNMENT 24

REMEDIES

NOTES

Insert on p. 816, after Note 8:

9. *Remedies against the State.* As noted in this Supplement (Assignments 5 and 13), on the last day of October Term 1998, the Supreme Court issued a trio of opinions extending the reach of state sovereign immunity. These cases may make it very difficult to control intellectual property infringements committed by a state or one of its arms. For our purposes, the most important of these cases is Florida Prepaid Postsecondary Education Expense Board v. College Savings Bank,[1] which held that College Savings cannot rely on the Patent Remedy Clarification Act ("PRCA"),[2] in which Congress waived state sovereign immunity to patent suits, to bring an action for monetary damages against Florida on account of its infringement of College Savings' patent on a method for financing future college expenses. Although the Court acknowledged that courts have traditionally recognized patents as a form of property, and that Congress has authority under the Enforcement Clause of the Fourteenth Amendment to waive state immunity from suit with "appropriate" legislation, it did not consider the PRCA appropriate, at least not without further congressional findings that other forms of relief are insufficient.

The need for specific findings is somewhat curious, given that the availability of other forms of relief against the states is clearly quite limited. Patent infringement is now solely within the jurisdiction of federal courts.[3] Congress could change the jurisdiction rule to provide for concurrent state and federal authority over patent law, but that course might threaten the uniform administration of patent policy. Moreover, in a companion case, Alden v. Maine,[4] the Court made this approach unavailable. *Alden* held that Congress cannot waive a state's sovereign immunity in its own state courts on federal causes of action for money damages. And given the strong preemption doctrines that we saw in Assignment 14 and that we will see in Assignment 25, neither will it be easy to create state-law analogues to patent infringement that will withstand preemption. While a suit in federal court for injunctive relief remains an option, there is a

[1] ___ U.S. ___, 119 S.Ct. 2199, ___ L.Ed.2d ___ (1999).

[2] 35 U.S.C. § 296.

[3] 28 U.S.C. § 1338.

[4] ___ U.S. ___, 119 S.Ct. 2240, ___ L.Ed.2d ___ (1999).

question whether patentees will be able to afford to bring such actions without the prospect of a monetary return. (Even the possibility of being awarded attorneys fees is a question after these cases, although they might be available if considered equitable.[5]) There is also reason to doubt that an action for injunctive relief will provide sufficient deterrence. For example, in biomedical research, the biological activity of molecules can be related to their shape. Knowing the shape of one bioactive agent can therefore be helpful in designing another. Under *Florida Prepaid*, researchers at state universities will now be able to use patented molecules as a basis for their own research. Although they may be sued for infringement, their need for access to the patented technology may have ended by the time injunctive relief is granted and the use itself will not require compensation because of the state's sovereign immunity. Will, then, *Florida Prepaid* distort the market for technological research by giving researchers at state universities an important advantage? The Supreme Court argued that there has only been a "handful of instances of state patent infringement." However, as Justice Stevens pointed out in dissent, the Court failed to consider the many cases involving just this issue: infringement at state universities.

[5] See § 285 (citing to "principles of equity").

ASSIGNMENT 25

PREEMPTION OF STATE LAWS: TRADE SECRETS, COVENANTS NOT TO COMPETE, AND LEGAL HYBRIDS

Insert at page 826, after *Gillette*:

Pepsico, Inc. v. Redmond

United States Court of Appeals, Seventh Circuit, 1995.
54 F.3d 1262.

■ FLAUM, CIRCUIT JUDGE.

Plaintiff PepsiCo, Inc., sought a preliminary injunction against defendants William Redmond and the Quaker Oats Company to prevent Redmond, a former PepsiCo employee, from divulging PepsiCo trade secrets and confidential information in his new job with Quaker and from assuming any duties with Quaker relating to beverage pricing, marketing, and distribution. The district court agreed with PepsiCo and granted the injunction. We now affirm that decision.

I

The facts of this case lay against a backdrop of fierce beverage-industry competition between Quaker and PepsiCo, especially in "sports drinks" and "new age drinks." Quaker's sports drink, "Gatorade," is the dominant brand in its market niche. PepsiCo introduced its Gatorade rival, "All Sport," in March and April of 1994, but sales of All Sport lag far behind those of Gatorade. Quaker also has the lead in the new-age-drink category. Although PepsiCo has entered the market through joint ventures with the Thomas J. Lipton Company and Ocean Spray Cranberries, Inc., Quaker purchased Snapple Beverage Corp., a large new-age-drink maker, in late 1994. PepsiCo's products have about half of Snapple's market share. Both companies see 1995 as an important year for their products: PepsiCo has developed extensive plans to increase its market presence, while Quaker is trying to solidify its lead by integrating Gatorade and Snapple distribution. Meanwhile, PepsiCo and Quaker each face strong competition from Coca Cola Co., which has its own sports drink, "PowerAde," and which introduced its own Snapple-rival, "Fruitopia," in 1994, as well as from independent beverage producers.

William Redmond, Jr., worked for PepsiCo in its Pepsi–Cola North America division ("PCNA") from 1984 to 1994. Redmond became the General Manager of the Northern California Business Unit in June, 1993, and was promoted one year later to General Manager of the business unit covering all of California, a unit having annual revenues of more than 500 million dollars and representing twenty percent of PCNA's profit for all of the United States.

Redmond's relatively high-level position at PCNA gave him access to inside information and trade secrets. Redmond, like other PepsiCo management employees, had signed a confidentiality agreement with PepsiCo. That agreement stated in relevant part that he

> w[ould] not disclose at any time, to anyone other than officers or employees of [PepsiCo], or make use of, confidential information relating to the business of [PepsiCo] . . . obtained while in the employ of [PepsiCo], which shall not be generally known or available to the public or recognized as standard practices.

Donald Uzzi, who had left PepsiCo in the beginning of 1994 to become the head of Quaker's Gatorade division, began courting Redmond for Quaker in May, 1994. Redmond met in Chicago with Quaker officers in August, 1994, and on October 20, 1994, Quaker, through Uzzi, offered Redmond the position of Vice President—On Premise Sales for Gatorade. Redmond did not then accept the offer but continued to negotiate for more money. Throughout this time, Redmond kept his dealings with Quaker secret from his employers at PCNA.

On November 8, 1994, Uzzi extended Redmond a written offer for the position of Vice President–Field Operations for Gatorade and Redmond accepted. Later that same day, Redmond called William Bensyl, the Senior Vice President of Human Resources for PCNA, and told him that he had an offer from Quaker to become the Chief Operating Officer of the combined Gatorade and Snapple company but had not yet accepted it. Redmond also asked whether he should, in light of the offer, carry out his plans to make calls upon certain PCNA customers. Bensyl told Redmond to make the visits.

Redmond also misstated his situation to a number of his PCNA colleagues, including Craig Weatherup, PCNA's President and Chief Executive Officer, and Brenda Barnes, PCNA's Chief Operating Officer and Redmond's immediate superior. As with Bensyl, Redmond told them that he had been offered the position of Chief Operating Officer at Gatorade and that he was leaning "60/40" in favor of accepting the new position.

On November 10, 1994, Redmond met with Barnes and told her that he had decided to accept the Quaker offer and was resigning from PCNA.

Barnes immediately took Redmond to Bensyl, who told Redmond that PepsiCo was considering legal action against him.

True to its word, PepsiCo filed this diversity suit on November 16, 1994, seeking a temporary restraining order to enjoin Redmond from assuming his duties at Quaker and to prevent him from disclosing trade secrets or confidential information to his new employer. From November 23, 1994, to December 1, 1994, the district court conducted a preliminary injunction hearing on the same matter. At the hearing, PepsiCo offered evidence of a number of trade secrets and confidential information it desired protected and to which Redmond was privy. First, it identified PCNA's "Strategic Plan," an annually revised document that contains PCNA's plans to compete, its financial goals, and its strategies for manufacturing, production, marketing, packaging, and distribution for the coming three years. Strategic Plans are developed by Weatherup and his staff with input from PCNA's general managers, including Redmond, and are considered highly confidential. The Strategic Plan derives much of its value from the fact that it is secret and competitors cannot anticipate PCNA's next moves. PCNA managers received the most recent Strategic Plan at a meeting in July, 1994, a meeting Redmond attended. PCNA also presented information at the meeting regarding its plans for Lipton ready-to-drink teas and for All Sport for 1995 and beyond, including new flavors and package sizes.

Second, PepsiCo pointed to PCNA's Annual Operating Plan ("AOP") as a trade secret. The AOP is a national plan for a given year and guides PCNA's financial goals, marketing plans, promotional event calendars, growth expectations, and operational changes in that year. The AOP, which is implemented by PCNA unit General Managers, including Redmond, contains specific information regarding all PCNA initiatives for the forthcoming year. The AOP bears a label that reads "Private and Confidential— Do Not Reproduce" and is considered highly confidential by PCNA managers.

In particular, the AOP contains important and sensitive information about "pricing architecture"—how PCNA prices its products in the marketplace. Pricing architecture covers both a national pricing approach and specific price points for given areas. Pricing architecture also encompasses PCNA's objectives for All Sport and its new age drinks with reference to trade channels, package sizes and other characteristics of both the products and the customers at which the products are aimed. Additionally, PCNA's pricing architecture outlines PCNA's customer development agreements. These agreements between PCNA and retailers provide for the retailer's participation in certain merchandising activities for PCNA products. As with other information contained in the AOP, pricing architecture is highly confidential and would be extremely valuable to a competitor. Knowing PCNA's pricing architecture would allow a competitor to anticipate PCNA's pricing moves and underbid PCNA strategically whenever and wherever the competitor so desired. PepsiCo introduced evidence that Redmond had detailed knowledge of PCNA's pricing architecture and that he was aware of and had been involved in preparing PCNA's customer development agreements with PCNA's California and California-based national customers. Indeed, PepsiCo showed that Redmond, as the General Manager for California, would have been responsible for implementing the pricing architecture guidelines for his business unit.

PepsiCo also showed that Redmond had intimate knowledge of PCNA "attack plans" for specific markets. Pursuant to these plans, PCNA dedicates extra funds to supporting its brands against other brands in selected markets. To use a hypothetical example, PCNA might budget an additional $500,000 to spend in Chicago at a particular time to help All Sport close its market gap with Gatorade. Testimony and documents demonstrated Redmond's awareness of these plans and his participation in drafting some of them.

Finally, PepsiCo offered evidence of PCNA trade secrets regarding innovations in its selling and delivery systems. Under this plan, PCNA is testing a new delivery system that could give PCNA an advantage over its competitors in negotiations with retailers over shelf space and merchandising. Redmond has knowledge of this secret because PCNA, which has invested over a million dollars in developing the system during the past two years, is testing the pilot program in California.

Having shown Redmond's intimate knowledge of PCNA's plans for 1995, PepsiCo argued that Redmond would inevitably disclose that information to Quaker in his new position, at which he would have substantial input as to Gatorade and Snapple pricing, costs, margins, distribution systems, products, packaging and marketing, and could give Quaker an unfair advantage in its upcoming skirmishes with PepsiCo. Redmond and Quaker countered that Redmond's primary initial duties at Quaker as Vice President—Field Operations would be to integrate Gatorade and Snapple distribution and then to manage that distribution as well as the promotion, marketing and sales of these products. Redmond asserted that the integration would be conducted according to a pre-existing plan and that his special knowledge of PCNA strategies would be irrelevant. This irrelevance would derive not only from the fact that Redmond would be implementing pre-existing plans but also from the fact that PCNA and Quaker distribute their products in entirely different ways: PCNA's distribution system is vertically integrated (i.e., PCNA owns the system) and delivers its product directly to retailers, while Quaker ships its product to wholesalers and customer warehouses and relies on independent distributors. The defendants also pointed out that Redmond had signed a confidentiality agreement with Quaker preventing him from disclosing "any confidential information belonging to others," as well as the Quaker Code of Ethics, which prohibits employees from engaging in "illegal or improper acts to acquire a competitor's trade secrets." Redmond additionally promised at the hearing that should he be faced with a situation at Quaker that might involve the use or disclosure of PCNA information, he would seek advice from Quaker's in-house counsel and would refrain from making the decision.

PepsiCo responded to the defendants' representations by pointing out that the evidence did not show that Redmond would simply be implementing a business plan already in place. On the contrary, as of November, 1994, the plan to integrate Gatorade and Snapple distribution consisted of a single distributorship agreement and a two-page "contract terms summary." Such a basic plan would not lend itself to widespread application among the over 300 independent Snapple distributors. Since the integration process would likely face resistance from Snapple distributors and Quaker had no scheme to deal with this probability, Redmond, as the person in charge of the integration, would likely have a great deal of influence on the process. PepsiCo further argued that Snapple's 1995 marketing and promotion plans had not necessarily been completed prior to Redmond's joining Quaker, that Uzzi disagreed with portions of the Snapple plans, and that the plans were open to re-evaluation. Uzzi testified that the plan for integrating Gatorade and Snapple distribution is something that would happen in the future. Redmond would therefore likely have input in remaking these plans, and if he did, he would inevitably be making decisions with PCNA's strategic plans and 1995 AOP in mind. Moreover, PepsiCo continued, diverging testimony made it difficult to know exactly what Redmond would be doing at Quaker. Redmond described his job as "managing the entire sales effort of Gatorade at the field level, possibly including strategic planning," and at least at one point considered his job to be equivalent to that of a Chief Operating Officer. Uzzi, on the other hand, characterized Redmond's position as "primarily and initially to restructure and integrate our—the distribution systems for Snapple and for Gatorade, as per our distribution plan" and then to "execute marketing, promotion and sales plans in the marketplace." Uzzi also denied having given Redmond detailed information about any business plans, while Redmond described such a plan in depth in an affidavit and said that he received the information from Uzzi. Thus, PepsiCo asserted, Redmond would have a high position in the Gatorade hierarchy, and PCNA trade secrets and confidential information would necessarily influence his decisions. Even if Redmond could somehow refrain from relying on this information, as he promised he would, his actions in leaving PCNA, Uzzi's actions in hiring Redmond, and the varying testimony regarding Redmond's new responsibilities, made Redmond's assurances to PepsiCo less than comforting.

On December 15, 1994, the district court issued an order enjoining Redmond from assuming his position at Quaker through May, 1995, and permanently from using or disclosing any PCNA trade secrets or confidential information. The court entered its findings of fact and conclusions of law on January 26, 1995, nunc pro tunc December 15, 1994. The court, which completely adopted PepsiCo's position, found that Redmond's new job posed a clear threat of misappropriation of trade secrets and confidential information that could be enjoined under Illinois statutory and common law. The court also emphasized Redmond's lack of forthrightness both in his activities before accepting his job with Quaker and in his testimony as factors leading the court to believe the threat of misappropriation was real. This appeal followed.

II

A

The Illinois Trade Secrets Act ("ITSA"), which governs the trade secret issues in this case, provides that a court may enjoin the "actual or threatened misappropriation" of a trade secret. 765 ILCS 1065/3(a); George S. May Int'l Co. v. Int'l Profit Associates, 256 Ill.App.3d 779, 195 Ill.Dec. 183, 189, 628 N.E.2d 647, 653 (1st Dist.1993), appeal denied, 156 Ill.2d 557, 202 Ill.Dec. 921, 638 N.E.2d 1115 (1994); see also 2 Melvin F. Jager, Trade Secrets Law § IL.01[7] at IL–7 to 8 (Clark Boardman Callaghan, rev. ed. 1994). A party seeking an injunction must therefore prove both the existence of a trade secret and the misappropriation. The defendants' appeal focuses solely on misappropriation; although the defendants only reluctantly refer to PepsiCo's marketing and distribution plans as trade secrets, they do not seriously contest that this information falls under the ITSA.

The question of threatened or inevitable misappropriation in this case lies at the heart of a basic tension in trade secret law. Trade secret law serves to protect "standards of commercial morality" and "encourage [ ] invention and innovation" while maintaining "the public interest in having free and open competition in the manufacture and sale of unpatented goods." 2 Jager, supra, § IL.03 at IL–12. Yet that same law should not prevent workers from pursuing their livelihoods when they leave their current positions. American Can Co. v. Mansukhani, 742 F.2d 314, 329 (7th Cir.1984).

This tension is particularly exacerbated when a plaintiff sues to prevent not the actual misappropriation of trade secrets but the mere threat that it will occur. While the ITSA plainly permits a court to enjoin the threat of misappropriation of trade secrets, there is little law in Illinois or in this circuit establishing what constitutes threatened or inevitable misappropriation. Indeed, there are only two cases in this circuit that address the issue: Teradyne, Inc. v. Clear Communications Corp., 707 F.Supp. 353 (N.D.Ill 1989), and AMP Inc. v. Fleischhacker, 823 F.2d 1199 (7th Cir. 1987). [These cases and the ITSA] lead to the same conclusion: a plaintiff may prove a claim of trade secret misappropriation by demonstrating that defendant's new employment will inevitably lead him to rely on the plaintiff's trade secrets. See also 1 Jager, supra, § 7.02[2][a] at 7–20 (noting claims where "the allegation is based on the fact that the disclosure of trade secrets in the new employment is inevitable, whether or not the former employee acts consciously or unconsciously"). The defendants are incorrect that Illinois law does not allow a court to enjoin the "inevitable" disclosure of trade secrets. Questions remain, however, as to what constitutes inevitable misappropriation and whether PepsiCo's submissions rise above those of the Teradyne and AMP plaintiffs and meet that standard. We hold that they do.

PepsiCo presented substantial evidence at the preliminary injunction hearing that Redmond possessed extensive and intimate knowledge about PCNA's strategic goals for 1995 in sports drinks and new age drinks. The district court concluded on the basis of that presentation that unless Redmond possessed an uncanny ability to compartmentalize information, he would necessarily be making decisions about Gatorade and Snapple by relying on his knowledge of PCNA trade secrets. It is not the "general skills and knowledge acquired during his tenure with" PepsiCo that PepsiCo seeks to keep from falling into Quaker's hands, but rather "the particularized plans or processes developed by [PCNA] and disclosed to him while the employer-employee relationship existed, which are unknown to others in the industry and which give the employer an advantage over his competitors." AMP, 823 F.2d at 1202. The Teradyne and AMP plaintiffs could do nothing more than assert that skilled employees were taking their skills elsewhere; PepsiCo has done much more.

Admittedly, PepsiCo has not brought a traditional trade secret case, in which a former employee has knowledge of a special manufacturing process or customer list and can give a competitor an unfair advantage by transferring the technology or customers to that competitor. See, e.g., Glenayre Electronics, Ltd. v. Sandahl, 830 F.Supp. 1149 (C.D.Ill. 1993) (preliminary injunction sought to prevent use of trade secrets regarding pager technology). PepsiCo has not contended that Quaker has stolen the All Sport formula or its list of distributors. Rather PepsiCo has asserted that Redmond cannot help but rely on PCNA trade secrets as he helps plot Gatorade and Snapple's new course, and that these secrets will enable Quaker to achieve a substantial advantage by knowing exactly how PCNA will price, distribute, and market its sports drinks and new age drinks and being able to respond strategically. cf. FMC Corp. v. Varco Int'l, Inc., 677 F.2d 500, 504 (5th Cir.1982) ("Even assuming the best of good faith, Witt will have difficulty preventing his knowledge of FMC's 'Longsweep' manufacturing techniques from infiltrating his work."). This type of trade secret problem may arise less often, but it nevertheless falls within the realm of trade secret protection under the present circumstances.

Quaker and Redmond assert that they have not and do not intend to use whatever confidential information Redmond has by virtue of his former employment. They point out that Redmond has already signed an agreement with Quaker not to disclose any trade secrets or confidential information gleaned from his earlier employment. They also note with regard to distribution systems that even if Quaker wanted to steal information about

PCNA's distribution plans, they would be completely useless in attempting to integrate the Gatorade and Snapple beverage lines.

The defendants' arguments fall somewhat short of the mark. Again, the danger of misappropriation in the present case is not that Quaker threatens to use PCNA's secrets to create distribution systems or co-opt PCNA's advertising and marketing ideas. Rather, PepsiCo believes that Quaker, unfairly armed with knowledge of PCNA's plans, will be able to anticipate its distribution, packaging, pricing, and marketing moves. Redmond and Quaker even concede that Redmond might be faced with a decision that could be influenced by certain confidential information that he obtained while at PepsiCo. In other words, PepsiCo finds itself in the position of a coach, one of whose players has left, playbook in hand, to join the opposing team before the big game. Quaker and Redmond's protestations that their distribution systems and plans are entirely different from PCNA's are thus not really responsive.

The district court also concluded from the evidence that Uzzi's actions in hiring Redmond and Redmond's actions in pursuing and accepting his new job demonstrated a lack of candor on their part and proof of their willingness to misuse PCNA trade secrets, findings Quaker and Redmond vigorously challenge. The facts of the case do not ineluctably dictate the district court's conclusion. Redmond's ambiguous behavior toward his PepsiCo superiors might have been nothing more than an attempt to gain leverage in employment negotiations. The discrepancy between Redmond's and Uzzi's comprehension of what Redmond's job would entail may well have been a simple misunderstanding. The court also pointed out that Quaker, through Uzzi, seemed to express an unnatural interest in hiring PCNA employees: all three of the people interviewed for the position Redmond ultimately accepted worked at PCNA. Uzzi may well have focused on recruiting PCNA employees because he knew they were good and not because of their confidential knowledge. Nonetheless, the district court, after listening to the witnesses, determined otherwise. That conclusion was not an abuse of discretion.

Thus, when we couple the demonstrated inevitability that Redmond would rely on PCNA trade secrets in his new job at Quaker with the district court's reluctance to believe that Redmond would refrain from disclosing these secrets in his new position (or that Quaker would ensure Redmond did not disclose them), we conclude that the district court correctly decided that PepsiCo demonstrated a likelihood of success on its statutory claim of trade secret misappropriation.

· · ·

C

For the same reasons we concluded that the district court did not abuse its discretion in granting the preliminary injunction on the issue of trade secret misappropriation, we also agree with its decision on the likelihood of Redmond's breach of his confidentiality agreement should he begin working at Quaker. Because Redmond's position at Quaker would initially cause him to disclose trade secrets, it would necessarily force him to breach his agreement not to disclose confidential information acquired while employed in PCNA. Cf. George S. May Int'l, 195 Ill.Dec. at 189, 628 N.E.2d at 653 ("An employer's trade secrets are considered a protectable interest for a restrictive covenant under Illinois law.").

Quaker and Redmond do not assert that the confidentiality agreement is invalid; such agreements are enforceable when supported by adequate consideration. See, e.g, Corroon & Black of Illinois, Inc. v. Magner, 145 Ill.App.3d 151, 98 Ill.Dec. 663, 669, 494 N.E.2d 785, 791 (1st Dist.1986). Rather, they argue that "inevitable" breaches of these contracts may not be enjoined. The case on which they rely, however, R.R. Donnelley & Sons Co. v. Fagan, 767 F.Supp. 1259 (S.D.N.Y.1991) (applying Illinois law), says nothing of the sort. The R.R. Donnelley court merely found that the plaintiffs had failed to prove the existence of any confidential information or any indication that the defendant would ever use it. Id. at 1267. The threat of misappropriation that drives our holding with regard to trade secrets dictates the same result here.

III

. . .

For the foregoing reasons, we affirm the district court's order enjoining Redmond from assuming his responsibilities at Quaker through May, 1995, and preventing him forever from disclosing PCNA trade secrets and confidential information.

NOTES

Insert at page 843, after Note 1c.:

d. *Criminal law.* In 1996, Congress strengthened the protection of trade secrets by recognizing a new federal crime of economic espionage. The definition of a trade secret in the Economic Espionage Act[1] mirrors that of typical state laws. However, the Act is broader than state trade secrecy laws in many other respects. It contains an expansive definition of misappropriation, including such actions as unauthorized copying, duplicating, sketching, drawing, photographing, downloading, uploading, altering, destroying, photocopying, replicating, transmitting, delivering, sending, mailing, communicating, or conveying a trade secret; it criminalizes attempts and conspiracies; and—unlike most intellectual property laws—it reaches extraterritorial activity whenever the offender is a U.S. citizen, a resident alien, or is organized under the laws of the U.S. or a state, and also when an activity in furtherance of the offense is committed in the U.S. Punishment, which depends on whether the intended beneficiary is a

---

[1] 18 U.S.C. § 1831–39.

foreign government or a private party, includes fines up to $500,000, imprisonment up to 15 years (or both), as well as forfeiture of property used to commit the crime or derived as a result of the crime. The economic proceeds of a conviction go to the government, not the target of the espionage. However, the prosecutor can aid the target by bringing an action for injunctive relief.

Despite its breadth, the Act does have a few limiting features. First, it can only be enforced by the government; until 2001, the permission of the Attorney General or one of the top two deputies in the Justice Department is required to initiate a prosecution. Second, the Act has several important scienter requirements. For example, in cases involving private party beneficiaries, the prosecutor must show that the defendant intended to convert a trade secret and intended to benefit someone other than the owner, had intent or knowledge that the information will injure an owner of the trade secret, and knew that she was engaged in a denominated act of misappropriation. Third, as with all criminal statutes, the prosecution must prove its case beyond a reasonable doubt.

It is not, however, clear that these limitations go far enough. Consider, for example, the activities that were undertaken in *Sega v. Accolade*, Assignment 10, Note 9, page 409 of the casebook, in order to produce game cassettes that work on Sega's game console: would such activities violate the Economic Espionage Act? The taking of information by proper means is not a crime, but the Act nowhere defines "proper." If interim copying is considered improper, then activities aimed at creating compatible products, or follow on inventions, could be punishable. Similarly, consider *PepsiCo v. Redmond*, supra: could Redmond be prosecuted for changing jobs? Given that organizations can also be prosecuted, how would you have advised Quaker on the question whether it should have hired Redmond in the first place? The legislative history of the Act expresses concern about chilling employee mobility, but the Act contains no special protection for either employers or employees. As a result, lawyers are advising clients to adopt rigorous screening requirements and procedures to insulate new employees from projects that would benefit from their prior experience.[2] Is this a felicitous way to optimize the flow of information? To maintain salaries in the innovation sector?

The one case reported to date is also less than comforting. United States v. Hsu[3] was a sting operation mounted against individuals suspected of trying to steal BristolMyers Squibb's trade secrets for manufacturing Taxol, an important anticancer drug. After "dummy technology" (that is, not the real trade secret) was passed, the individuals were charged with

---

[2] See, e.g., James H.A. Pooley, Mark A. Lemley, Peter J. Toren, Understanding the Economic Espionage Act of 1996, 5 Tex. Intell. Prop. L.J. 177, 217–18 (1997); Gerald J. Mossinghoff, J. Derek Mason, David A. Oblon, The Economic Espionage Act: A New Federal Regime of Trade Secret Protection, 79 J. Pat. & Trademark Off. Soc'y 191, 192 (1997).

[3] 155 F.3d 189 (3d Cir. 1998).

violating the Economic Espionage Act. The defendants sought discovery on the taxol method in order to defend on the ground of impossibility—that is, on the ground that the information that they intended to take was not a trade secret. The district court agreed, but the Third Circuit reversed, stating:

> A defendant is guilty of attempting to misappropriate trade secrets if, "acting with the kind of culpability otherwise required for commission of the crime, he ... purposely does or omits to do anything that, under the circumstances as he believes them to be, is an act or omission constituting a substantial step in a course of conduct planned to culminate in his commission of the crime." Model Penal Code § 5.01(1)(c) (1985). Thus, the defendant must (1) have the intent needed to commit a crime defined by the EEA, and must (2) perform an act amounting to a "substantial step" toward the commission of that crime.... The government can satisfy its burden under § 1832(a)(4) by proving beyond a reasonable doubt that the defendant sought to acquire information which he or she believed to be a trade secret, regardless of whether the information actually qualified as such.[4]

Insert at page 849, at the end of the last paragraph in Note 8:

With the rise in the use of trade dress law to protect product configurations, see Assignment 3, courts have become more aggressive in using a preemption analysis to protect the accessibility of nonpatented products. For example, in Vornado Air Circulation Systems, Inc. v. Duracraft Corp.,[5] the Tenth Circuit held that a the novel grill design of a household fan could not be protected under § 43(a) of the Lanham Act on the ground that federal patent and copyright policy required that it remain in the public domain. See also Assignment 3, Note 5, supra (in this Supplement).

Add on page 849, after Note 8:

9. *Private alternatives to patent and trade secrecy protection.* As noted in the supplemental material for page 550, *supra,* Assignment 14, the National Conference of Commissioners on Uniform State Law (NCCUSL) is considering the promulgation of the Uniform Computer Information Transactions Act (UCITA). Although in its present form, the Act deals mainly with software sales and licensing, and thus, copyright issues, the initiative could have broader impact. It will cover patents, trade secrets and other information subject to a duty of confidentiality that is related to software. Moreover, states could apply the Act by analogy to other licensing situations. Finally, parties could by agreement opt into its provisions.

---

[4] Id. at p. 202.

[5] 58 F.3d 1498 (10th Cir.1995), cert. denied, 516 U.S. 1067, 116 S.Ct. 753, 133 L.Ed.2d 700 (1996).

As in copyright, one question is whether the holder of an intellectual property right can "ratchet up" protection through a bilateral agreement without violating federal policy. For example, reconsider the cases on repair in Assignment 22, *Sandvik Aktiebolag, supra,* or *Aro Manufacturing Co.,* on page 749 of the casebook. Both cases held that in some circumstances, restoring features of a patented invention is not infringement. Should a licensor be allowed to limit this right to repair through contractual agreement? In Mallinckrodt, Inc. v. Medipart, Inc.,[6] the Federal Circuit indicated that there are circumstances where such limitations are permissible. However, that case involved medical syringes and concerns about safety; UCITA would facilitate the imposition of such restrictions in other circumstances.

A second question is whether information that is not subject to patent can be protected contractually. For example, we have just seen that trade secrets survive preemption challenge because they can always be reverse engineered. But what if a product containing nonpublic information is licensed rather than sold, and the licensing agreement prohibits the licensee from reverse engineering? Will the license violate *Bonito Boats*? Does a state law that facilitates such a license violate *Bonito Boats*? The drafters of UCITA argue that a right that runs against an individual is not the same as a right—such as a statutory ban on plug molds—that runs against the world. Do you read *Bonito Boats* this way? If it becomes easy to license technology, will anyone pay the cost of obtaining a patent? Will the statute then violate *Kewanee Oil*? In this regard, note that licenses under UCITA can run perpetually. Even after they are breached or expire, duties of confidentiality and certain restrictions on use may remain in force.

A final question about UCITA is whether it can, consistent with federal law, facilitate the licensing of *public* information. On the whole, the line that UCITA draws is between information that is subject to a duty of confidentiality and information that is not subject to such a duty—not the line that trade secrecy law draws between information that is public and information that is valuable because it is secret. Do agreements to pay royalties on account of public information—or a statute that facilitates such agreements—violate *Kewanee* or *Bonito Boats*? The drafters argue that licenses for "black art"—that is, information whose status as secret or public is not known—are common in the technology sector. The licensee needs the information, is eager to learn it from the licensor at the price that the licensor is charging, and neither side wants to incur the cost of determining whether the information is secret or not. Should such an arrangement be characterized as a license for information or is it really a contract to pay tuition for instruction?

10. *Vessel Hulls.* As noted earlier in this Supplement (in the Note for page 316), Congress has now enacted federal legislation to protect boat hulls. Paradoxically, this legislation is actually broader than the Act at issue in

[6] 976 F.2d 700 (Fed. Cir. 1992).

Bonito Boats, for it protects both the hulls made with a plug mold and the plug mold. Is this law constitutional? In addition to reviewing *Bonito Boats*, consider Feist Publications, Inc. v. Rural Telephone Service Co., Inc., in Assignment 7.

11. *Licensing restrictions*. In ProCD Inc. v. Zeidenberg,[7] the Seventh Circuit upheld a licensing restriction imposed on the use of a database inscribed on CDs, despite the fact that the database is not protectable under copyright law. How would this case change your answer to the Principal Problem?

[7] 86 F.3d 1447 (7th Cir.1996).

†

ISBN 1-56662-810-5

90000

9 781566 628105